Managing Anger Through Selfless Thinking

Floyd F. Robison, Ph.D.
Indiana University

James Ervin Publications
Beaverton, Oregon

Copyright 2007 by James Ervin Publications. All rights reserved. Printed in the United States of America. Except as permitted under the United States Copyright Act of 1976, no part of this publication may be reproduced or redistributed in any form or by any means, or stored in a database or retrieval system, without the prior written permission of the publisher.

1. Self Improvement

ISBN: 978-0-6151-6044-3

James Ervin Publications

14525 S.W. Millikan Way, Suite 47630

Beaverton, OR 97005 - 2343

Table of Contents

Preface		v
Chapter 1:	Purpose of this Book	9
Chapter 2:	Why People Get Angry	17
Chapter 3:	Why Anger Gets Out of Control	23
Chapter 4:	Managing Anger in the Moment	35
Chapter 5:	The Selfless Lifestyle	45
Chapter 6:	Long-Term Anger Management	57
Chapter 7:	Relaxation and Stress Management	75
Chapter 8:	Case Examples	91
Epilogue		101
Appendix A:	Anger Management Worksheet	103
Appendix B:	Personal Goal-Setting Worksheet	107
About the Author		109
Index		111

Preface

This book is based on my work with patients in private practice and community counseling agencies since 1982, as well as my research on anger management as a faculty member at Indiana University. It is intended primarily to be a reference and workbook for persons who need a way to manage their anger. It also is intended to be a resource for professionals who provide anger management services. These professionals include counselors, social workers, psychologists, corrections specialists, medical personnel, and clergy. The techniques presented here are straightforward. Although they are based in established theories and research on anger control, they have been adjusted to meet the needs of my own patients over the years.

There are many anger management books on the market, representing several schools of thought in psychology. Most of them are based on sound principles and readers will benefit from studying them. However, I have made some frequent observations in my clinical practice that led me to conclude another approach to anger management was needed for some people.

First, I observed that most anger management models are based on models that stress short-term changes in thought patterns and basic lifestyle behaviors (e.g., stress control, diet). These changes certainly are important. However, many people with poor anger control have what I call "angry personalities." They have deeply-rooted attitudes and beliefs that lead them to feel anger in most situations. Unless these attributes are changed, a chronically angry person is not likely to change much over time, even if that person learns specific anger control techniques. Those techniques become merely a bandage covering a deeper, unhealed wound.

Second, I have noticed that the most significant characteristic of angry personalities is a deep-seated narcissism or, put more simply, selfishness. Angry people may not be aware of their selfishness. Many of my patients in anger management therapy have protested that they are not selfish and described many occasions when they acted on others' behalf. Nonetheless, chronic, excessive anger is an expression of having placed one's needs, desires, or ideas before those of other people. Thus, in my treatment approach, chronically angry people must "get over themselves" by adopting what I call the selfless thinking style.

Third, I think that many anger management approaches do not place enough emphasis on personal responsibility for managing anger. Some approaches treat poor anger control as a mental disorder. I agree that some people do have mental disorders that limit their ability to manage strong emotion. However, I also believe that most people with poor anger management can easily, and rather quickly, make the changes necessary for them to manage anger successfully. They must take personal responsibility for their behavior and its consequences from the outset of their treatment in order to be successful. In fact, I consider unwillingness to always assume full responsibility for one's to be a characteristic of a selfish thinking style. Therefore, I repeatedly stress in this book the importance of taking personal responsibility for managing one's anger through the use of these techniques.

Finally, many anger management programs require months of counseling sessions. In my practice, patients learn the short-term anger control techniques described in this book within six weeks. Most of my patients complete the entire program within 12 weeks.

I want to thank my family for allowing me the time required to write a book. I also want to thank the clients who have completed this program and provided valuable feedback that enabled me to refine it.

Chapter 1
How Angry Are You?

Everyone gets angry. Anger is one of the four basic human emotions (the other three are fear, sadness, and joy). In fact, people who say they never become angry often have as much emotional distress as people who become angry too often. Anger can be a useful emotion because it makes us aware of situations when we may be in danger and should act to protect ourselves. The problem is not that people feel anger, but the actions they may take in response to their anger are inappropriate and interfere with the rights of others. The ability of people to express their anger in nonviolent, socially acceptable ways is called *anger management.*

How often do you get angry? How well do you deal with your anger? Do you have an anger management problem? Many people with this problem deny it. Sometimes, these people really don't know that their anger is out of control. Others know they have an anger problem but simply choose not to face the problem. To help you find out if you have a problem managing your anger successfully, answer each of the questions in the survey below. Answer each question as honestly as you can or you may ask a family member or friend you trust to complete the survey with you. When you have answered all the questions, add up your score and compare it to the scoring key.

Anger Management Quiz

_____ 1. I often get so angry it makes me feel physically ill.

_____ 2. In the past week, I have shouted at a person I care about, because I was angry.*

_____ 3. In the past month, I have broken something when I was angry.

_____ 4. I have been known to show "road rage."

_____ 5. In the past year, I have struck someone in anger*.

_____ 6. When I'm angry, everybody knows to "get out of the way."*

_____ 7. Anyone who challenges me is in for a quarrel.*

_____ 8. Some people are afraid of me because of my anger.*

_____ 9. Sometimes, people won't tell me things because they fear I'll get angry. *

_____ 10. I have been in trouble with the law because of my anger.

_____ 11. Loved ones have left me because of how I act when I'm angry.

_____ 12. I often regret what I did or said when I was angry.*

Give yourself one point for every "yes" answer." If you got a score of 0, congratulations! You don't have an anger management problem. If you scored between one and four points and you answered "no" to all the statements marked with a star (*), you may have some problems managing anger appropriately. If you got a score of five or higher or you answered "yes" to one or more statements marked with a star, you have a full-blown anger management problem. Your anger probably is causing great problems for you.

You're not alone. Anger management has become an important topic in society today. As a nation, we are becoming angrier and reacting to one another with increasing aggression. Episodes of road rage, once unknown on our highways and streets, have become common in many communities. Serious conflicts, ranging from fights at children's ball games to domestic violence, have increased steadily during the past 10 years.

There are several reasons for this increase in anger and the violence that comes with it. Some psychologists believe that uncontrolled anger is due to a high level of stress in our daily lives caused by numerous responsibilities, rapid advances in technology that cause information overload, and increasing demands of our jobs and families. Some psychologists believe that many people simply have poor self-discipline and exhibit rage as a form of temper tantrum when life doesn't go their way.

I'm particularly interested in the second explanation above. In my work with patients who have come to me for anger control therapy, I often find that they have difficulty with selfishness. They tend to put themselves first in most matters. They consider their ideas superior to those of others and are unwilling to consider other points of view during disagreements. In fact, they may find others' ideas to be threatening to them in various ways. They are impatient and, at times, impulsive. Perhaps most troubling, these people are disrespectful when they are selfish. They put others down and fail to recognize the basic worth of others.

What happens to people who don't manage their anger? If you're interested in this book, you may have experienced some of those consequences. Some of them are obvious. Excessively angry people who become violent are at risk to harm people or property and, thus, may have problems with the law. Excessive anger leads to serious relationship problems and, eventually, to loneliness if family members and friends avoid the angry person. Anger at work may lead to job demotions, disciplinary actions, and even firings. Basically, excessive anger leads to isolation from others.

But, there are others consequences of anger that you not have considered. Scientists have found that frequent, severe anger makes people physically ill. Severe anger has been linked to stomach disorders, ulcers, bowel disease, heart and vascular disease, headaches, chronic lower back and even muscular disorders. Uncontrolled anger may lead to mental health problems. These problems may include anxiety and depression, poor sleep, appetite difficulties, and even memory and thinking disorders. But, the most common and, in my opinion, most troubling consequence of uncontrolled anger is that an angry person simply is very unhappy. When a person is very angry much of the time, it is difficult to enjoy simply being alive. Angry people have a hard time appreciating the beauty of life and the goodness of those around them.

My method has both a short-term and long-term approach to managing anger. First, you will learn a specific technique for managing anger at times when you begin to lose control of your temper. This technique, described in Chapter 4, consists of four preliminary steps and five action steps that you will use when you feel your anger becoming out of control. Those techniques are simple and can be used whenever you need them.

However, I believe that truly effective long-term anger management cannot be achieved simply by using behavior change techniques each time someone is angry. Instead, successful long-term anger management requires one to make major changes in the way one thinks about others and why others act they as do. I call the outcome of these changes a *selfless thinking style.* Selfless people have attitudes that allow them to react to problems and conflicts without becoming highly angry. Their selfless attitudes enable them to manage their reactions easily when they are angered or feel any strong emotion.

In later chapters, I will present the personal characteristics, attitudes, and values that go along with a selfless thinking style. You will find examples of selfless thinking and self-talk to help you create your own selfless self-talk. I will also discuss habits that selfless people use to prevent anger from controlling them.

At the end of each chapter are questions and homework to help you apply the material in the chapter to your own situation. I encourage you to reflect on these questions and, furthermore, respond to them with the assistance of those persons (e.g., family, close friends) who will help you accomplish your anger management goals.

A word of caution is needed at this point, before reading further. *The anger management techniques presented in this book are not magic!* They are tools and nothing more. If you commit yourself to using them consistently, fully, and with complete intent to succeed, they will work in all but very few cases (which will be discussed in the next chapter). However, if you attempt to use these techniques half-heartedly or with the expectation that they will somehow magically transform you, I assure you that they will not work! Anger management requires your complete commitment to exploring the reasons for your anger and taking the steps to change consistently and fully. Put another way, you must take responsibility for managing anger, as you must take responsibility for all your actions.

Everyone can learn to control anger before it controls them. If you are ready to commit to a calmer lifestyle, good for you and best wishes! Read on . . .

Reflection Questions

1. In your own words, write down, or describe orally to a friend, the nature of your anger problem. What triggers your anger? How does your anger manifest itself? What do you say or do when your anger is out of control?

2. How does your anger problem affect your life at home, work, school, and the social organizations in which you participate? How has anger affected your relationships?

3. What are your three most important life goals? Write them down. Then, consider how has your anger problem has affected your progress to your goals? Have you had to change your goals because of your anger?

4. If you successfully gain control over your anger through this program, how will your life change in the family, school, work, and social areas during the next year, in five years, and in 10 years?

5. If you should choose not to learn gain control over your anger, describe what you think your life may be like in one, five, and 10 years.

6. After you have responded to questions 1 through 5, ask a trusted friend or family member to respond to them, based on their knowledge of you. Compare your responses with those from your friend or family member. In what ways are they similar and different? Do the similarities or differences surprise you? Why or why not?

Chapter 2
Why People Get Angry

Anger can be understood from the standpoints of biology and psychology. The biological viewpoint describes the physical mechanisms that produce anger, while the psychological viewpoint describes the mind's role in determining how one experiences and controls anger. In the following sections, we will explore the contributions of body and mind on the experience of anger.

The Biology of Anger

Believe it or not, all human emotions are the same from a biological standpoint. In the fifties and sixties, research on emotions led to the finding that emotions begin in certain structures deep within the human brain, collectively known as the *limbic system*. When stimulated, these structures produce hormones that cause a person to feel aroused. The stronger the stimulation of the limbic system, the stronger arousal a person tends to feel.

But how does this arousal translate into the experience of specific emotions? We interpret our physical arousal according to the circumstances that are taking place when we feel it. In other words, *we tell ourselves what we are feeling*. All emotions, joy, sadness, fear, and anger, begin merely as a state of general arousal produced by chemicals in the brain. People then label the arousal as a specific feeling *based upon what they tell themselves about what is happening around them*. Thus, if one becomes aroused in situations during which they do not like what is happening, or if they feel threatened or challenged, they may interpret their arousal as anger and react accordingly. But, if they experience arousal in those situations and interpret the situation in a positive way, they are likely to label their arousal as a more positive emotion. Again, they will react accordingly.

Self-Talk: the Psychology of Anger

There is a myth in our society that people who talk to themselves are crazy (and they're crazier if they answer themselves!). In fact, we all talk to ourselves! We simply don't talk out loud. Instead, we talk to ourselves within our heads as a running thought process. Anyone who spends much time around young children knows that they often talk aloud to themselves. As we grow into adulthood, our self-talk becomes an inner activity. We do not talk to ourselves aloud but we continue to have running conversations in our heads. Most people become so accustomed to their self-talk, they are not aware they are doing it. Psychologists have found that there is a strong connection between what people say to ourselves in any given situation and the emotions they feel in that situation. Certain types of self-talk have been linked with specific emotions.

Psychologist Aaron Beck[1] wrote that each of the major emotions are consistently associated with specific kinds of thoughts or self-talk. According to Beck, people feel anxiety in situations when they tell themselves that their world is being threatened or they may lose something important to them, and must find a way to rid themselves of the threat. They feel sadness when they think their world is being threatened and there is nothing they can do to stop the threat. They feel calm or even happiness when they tell themselves that they are in control of any threat and are able to bring about the outcomes they desire.

To illustrate how thoughts and emotions are connected, consider the following example:

Paul is an electrician. For the past several days, he has been wiring a house under construction in a local neighborhood. The job is complicated and he has spent many hours running cable, wiring the circuit breaker box, and checking connections. He is almost finished, which is good since he knows he must move on to wiring another house very soon in order to meet his commitments. This morning, however, the construction manager comes to Paul and tells him that the homeowner wants some changes in the wiring. These changes will require Paul to redo a substantial amount of the work he has done for the past few days and may make him have to delay the start of his next job. The construction manager insists that the changes must be made.

How will Paul feel? How will he react to the construction manager and others on the job site? It depends on what he tells himself about this situation and what he should do about it. Suppose he tells himself,

"This is crap! I've worked hard on this project, it's almost done, and I gotta move on!" The construction manager's supposed to keep this from happening, and he's taking the owner's side! This is stupid, completely out of line! If I don't finish this job and get to the

next house on time, I'll get canned! And like hell that's gonna happen!"

His self-talk probably will lead him to conclude that his world is being threatened and he will feel angry.

Once he feels his arousal as anger, he will tell himself what he should do. In the example above, Paul is likely to tell himself that he must fight in some way to stop the threat (in this case, the loss of his job or at least the loss of precious time). He will then react in ways that, according to his self-talk, will stop the threat. How aggressively he chooses to behave depends on what he typically tells himself that he should do in situations where his work is being threatened. He may tell himself that he must negotiate a solution with the foreman or, if he is feeling very angry, walk away from the site for a short time to calm himself. Or, his self-talk may lead him to shout at the foreman or even strike him.

Now, suppose that Paul tells himself something more hopeful about this situation. For example, suppose he says in his head,

"Oh man, this is gonna take some time, but I can make the time up on the next couple jobs. In the long run, the owner will be happier, the job probably will be better for the changes, and it'll be OK."

In this case, Paul will probably feel a more positive or hopeful emotion. He still may not be thrilled about the circumstances in which he finds himself, but he will not be nearly as angry as if he were thinking the thoughts in the first scene. Equally important, he will act in ways that work out the problems rather than fight out against the foreman.

Why People Get Angry

The diagram below shows the relationship between biological arousal, self-talk, feelings, and behavior in any given situation we encounter.

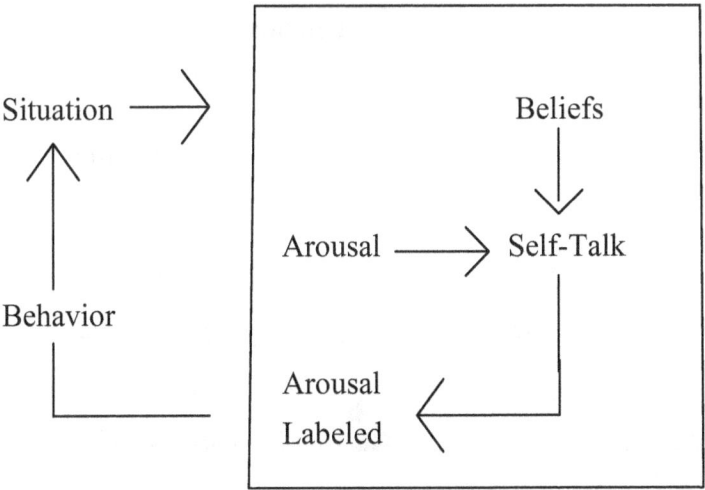

In this model, a person encounters a situation in which something happens (e.g., a conversation with someone or an event to which the person pays attention). The person feels arousal in reaction to the situation and engages in self-talk, telling oneself what is happening in the situation. The exact content of the self-talk is influenced by the person's beliefs. The self-talk allows the person to "feel" or label the arousal as an emotion (i.e., mad, sad, glad, or scared). Armed with this emotion and the self-talk that led to it, the person acts in particular ways. How the person acts will fit with how the person is feeling and telling herself or himself.

Reflection Questions

1. Reflect on two situations in which you tend to become angry. Write down the following information: (a) what happens in the

situation that makes you angry? (b) what do say to yourself when those circumstances occur. Be specific; *exactly* what do you say in your head? and (c) what do you do in these situations?

2. How do your actions relate to what you were telling yourself in your head? How do your feelings of anger relate to your self-talk in those situations?

3. As you were becoming angry, what kinds of messages did your body send you, to let you know that you were becoming angry?

4. Ask a trusted friend or family member to describe to you his or her observations as to what happens as you become angry? How does that person know you are getting angry? Compare this person's observations with your own impressions as to what happens when you get angry.

Reference Note

[1] Beck, Aaron (1976). *Cognitive therapy and the emotional disorders.*
New York: Basic Books.

Chapter 3
Why Anger Gets Out of Control

Psychologists have discovered that the people who have problems managing their anger tell themselves certain kinds of things about situations in which they feel threatened. These messages are called *angry self talk*. If people give these angry messages to themselves on a regular basis, in many types of situations, the self-messages are called *angry attitudes*. People who are troubled by angry attitudes are often angry all the time. Their attitudes direct them to react aggressively much of the time.

An important idea in this book is that angry attitudes are the products of a *selfish thinking style*. People who have anger control problems place themselves and their needs first. Others' needs and feelings are, quite simply, not important. If you dwell on having your way, believing that you are right and others are not, you are much more likely to believe that you have been slighted, ignored, attacked or not appreciated by others. Thus, you are likely to be angry often. The more frequently you become angry, the more likely your anger will become intense and hard to manage.

As I mentioned in the preceding chapter, another important idea in this book is that most people have the ability to take responsibility for their anger and manage it effectively if they wish to do so. However, a few people have mental and emotional conditions that hinder their ability to manage their anger successfully. These people may require additional help from a physician or therapist in addition to the anger management techniques in this book.

Types of Anger Self-Talk

Most angry self-talk comes from several beliefs that angry people have learned about the world. These beliefs can be understood in terms of general statements angry people say to themselves about situations in daily life and people in those situations. Not all angry people possess all of the beliefs, but most will harbor more than one within their views of the world. The most common angry self-talk statements are presented below:

"I'm better than everyone else; no one can tell me what to do or how things should be. I want what I want, period!"

Example: Ben had just finished writing a report for a project at work. His supervisor read the report, then politely asked Ben to make some changes in the wording of a few sections. Ben was proud of the way he written it and found his supervisor's criticism offensive. He thought to himself, "I know how to do this better than he, or anyone else does. How dare he criticize my work!" While his supervisor was talking to him, Ben threw the report in the trash and told the man off so loudly that he was heard throughout the office.

After many years of counseling angry people, I find that this is the most common reason for poor anger management. It is an utterly selfish attitude. People with this attitude look down on others and don't feel it necessary to treat others with respect. They become angry when they do not get their way or when they do not receive preferential treatment.

"I find your behavior directly threatening to me in some way and must react aggressively to stop the threat."

Example: Jane's neighbor came over to her apartment one evening to complain that her dog's barking is bothering her. The neighbor is very insulting and brings up the complex's rules on noise. She tells Jane, "If you don't make that dog stop barking right now, I'm calling the police!" Jane labels her arousal as anger because the neighbor may cause her to lose her beloved pet, her apartment, or both. Jane reacts to this threat by slapping the neighbor, in order to remove the source of the threat.

People who harbor this belief often have had life experiences during which they intimidated, threatened, or even abused. As children, they may have had aggressive parents who ruled by intimidation and expected them to respond aggressively in conflicts. In my clinical practice, I have noted that may adults who have had several significant personal losses during childhood and adolescence also tend to react aggressively in conflicts. They believe the conflict is another person's attempt to take something away from them. Their form of selfishness is that they are too sensitive to confrontation and too quick to fight off threats that, in fact, are not real.

"I believe that you are cheating or taking advantage of me, and I must fight back to protect my rights."

Example: Tom took his car to a local shop for an engine repair. The mechanic gave him an estimate of the cost to make the repair.

When Tom returned later that day, the mechanic presented him with a bill that was several dollars more than the estimated cost. The mechanic insisted that additional repairs had to be made in order for the car to run. Tom told himself that the additional repairs weren't necessary and certainly the mechanic should have known what work would be needed before starting the job. Thus, Tom believed that he was being cheated, thinking to himself, "No one cheats me and gets away with it!" He took a wrench from the mechanic's desk and threw it through a shop window.

People who harbor this belief often have parents who also believe that others cheat them. Such parents teach their children to believe, "Others will cheat you if you give them the chance."

Clearly, these are families who harbor much deep-seated mistrust of others and find the world a place from which one must protect oneself from thieves. The selfishness of this belief is that people believe that they are so important, so noticeable, that others would routinely *want* to cheat or steal from them. Most people have had the experience of being cheated or having someone take advantage of them. But, most of the time, no one is persistently a target of others' bad intentions.

"My authority is being challenged and this must not happen."

Example: Janet's four year-old son is marking on the wall with a crayon. Janet tells him to "stop that" and tries to take the crayon away. Her son resists, hanging on to the crayon saying, "You can't make me!" Janet feels her authority as a parent slipping away and tells herself, "No little brat is going to make me look bad. I'm the parent and my child will obey!" After a few moments, she screamed at the child, jerking the crayon from his hand.

The belief that one must be in control and confident throughout one's daily life is a common attitude contributing to strong anger. Many persons have been taught that adults should be in control of situations at all times. Although some people take this lesson to heart more than others, most people find themselves acting on the belief at least occasionally. The selfishness that accompanies a strong need for control is that controlling people ignore others' needs in order to remain in control. When others challenge a controlling person's authority, the controlling person tends to react in hostile ways.

There is another type of self-talk that may contribute to angry reactions when one's authority is challenged. Some people have become accustomed to being acknowledged as authority. Sometimes, these people may not actually have earned others' respect but others may "pretend" to defer to their so-called authority simply to appease them. When they do not receive this deference, whether real or imagined, they become angry and react with hostility.

"In some way, I'm failing or "not getting the job done."

Example: Frank has been working on an important project for his company. One afternoon, his supervisor came to his desk and criticized his work on a part of the project. As he listened to the criticism, Frank told himself that his boss was really calling him a failure, someone who couldn't really do his work correctly. Frank began to argue with his boss, disagreeing heatedly with his suggestions and finally demanding, "Get out of my office! Get some flunky to do your project!"

When people believe they are being confronted because they are failing, they show lack of self-confidence. They take offense at corrective feedback because they already are beating themselves up for not accomplishing tasks as they believe they ought to accomplish them. The selfishness of this self-talk is twofold. First, the person indirectly avoids responsibility for performing well by simply giving up on the task (i.e., I didn't get it right because I can't do it, so it's no use trying to learn how to do the task better in the future). Second, the person uses incompetence as an excuse to become angry at those who try to help, rather than use the help to improve performance.

"Anytime someone challenges you (or disagrees with you, or gets in your face), you better take care of it by fighting (or yelling, breaking something)."

Example: Carl is having a beer at a local tavern after work. On this day, he is talking about sports with one of the fellows by whom he often sits at the bar. The man criticizes Carl's opinion about the performance of a major league baseball player in a way that Carl takes as insulting. Believing that no one insults a real man, Carl beats the fellow unconscious.

Some of my anger management patients have told me quite bluntly, "Hey, if somebody gets in my face, I whip ass. That's what a man (woman) is supposed to do." Worldviews that include anger and aggression as gender functions (i.e., what men and women are supposed to do) almost always are the product of an antisocial upbringing. One or both parents have taught their children that aggression is an appropriate (or even required) response to conflict. In my work with clients, I have noticed that this self-talk tends to run in families. That is, generations of family members may respond to conflict in this manner. Unfortunately, in these same families, I have noticed that several family members may have served jail sentences or incurred other consequences, such as frequent job terminations, for antisocial behavior. The selfishness of people who have this attitude is that they place themselves above others, by concluding that they have the right to harm those who disagree with them.

"I can't control myself. My anger just happens all of a sudden and I do something aggressive before I realize it!"

Example: Anna was arrested for striking her husband with a brass lamp. This has been the third time she has hit him during an argument. When the judge asked her why she struck him, particularly after she had participated in counseling for anger management after the second incident, she replied, "Your Honor, I can't help myself. I get mad and, next thing I know, he's on the floor. I just can't stop myself. I just can't!"

Some psychologists refer to this type of thinking as *abdicating* (i.e., refusing to take) *responsibility*. Abdication is the selfishness of people with this attitude. These people refuse to take responsibility for controlling the thinking that leads them to feel angry, and the actions they take when they are angry. They insist that they "don't know" when they are becoming angry and can do nothing to control themselves. This is an excuse some angry people use to behave inappropriately without accepting the consequences of their behavior. Very few people are incapable of controlling their thinking and actions (and those people will be described in the next section). Most people can become aware of the physical cues and thoughts that will let them know when they are becoming angry, then take steps to manage their thinking and reactions to their anger.

Psychological Problems

Some people with anger management problems do, in fact, have other problems that hinder their success in controlling their anger. Even though these problems can make it more difficult to control anger, there is help for them. These problems are described below.

Depression and anxiety

People who suffer from depression and anxiety disorders may have greater difficulty managing anger. One of the symptoms of depression and anxiety can be increased anger. People who have these disorders feel the anger differently. Some find that they are irritable much of the time, while others may find that they "snap," or become enraged quite quickly and unexpectedly. When the underlying emotional problems are treated with a combination of psychotherapy and medication, the anger will improve. Thus, in order to fully succeed in anger management training, people with depressive and anxiety disorders should seek professional assistance to address all aspects of their emotional disturbances. With counseling and, when appropriate, medication to alleviate depression and anxiety, depressed can feel well, perform normally in daily activities, and manage their emotions effectively.

Impulse control disorders

Rarely, a person will have a psychiatric disorder that hinders the ability to manage aggressive impulses. One of these disorders is known as *bipolar disorder*. Bipolar disorder (once called manic-depressive disorder) has many types, but each type is characterized by periods of highs (mania) and lows (depression). The high and low periods vary in duration and intensity for different persons. Also, some persons experience the highs and lows in cycles, that is, they have a high period followed by a low period, possibly with a period of normal emotions and behaviors between the highs and lows. Some people may find that they have high and low periods at the same time.

Another impulse control disorder is known as Intermittent Explosive Disorder. People with this disorder go into rages unexpectedly, with little or no provocation. People with one of these disorders will need psychiatric help in order manage anger successfully. However, there are counseling procedures and psychiatric medications that are quite effective in helping impulsive people control themselves.

Personality disorders

Psychologists describe a personality disorder as persistent ways of thinking and behaving that are built into one's personality and causes problems for a person. Because these thoughts and behaviors are so much a part of the individual's personality, the individual often is unaware of those ways of thinking. Thus, the thoughts and behaviors can be quite difficult to change without intensive psychological counseling. Nonetheless, someone with a personality disorder has the ability to choose to change by entering counseling and committing to change thoughts and behaviors that cause poor anger management.

Psychotic disorders

Persons with psychiatric disorders such as *schizophrenia* may have increased anger and poor anger control as one of their symptoms. Anger problems are closely connected to the person's problems with thinking in an organized way. In some cases, the person may be reacting to hallucinations. However, most people with psychotic disorders obtain relief from a combination of psychiatric medications and counseling to help them manage their anger.

Low intelligence

In some cases (again, these are rare), a person who has low intelligence may have anger management problems. Someone with a mild intellectual handicap usually will not have more difficulty than someone with average intelligence in controlling anger. However, some people with moderate, severe, or profound intellectual handicaps may have much difficulty managing anger and other strong emotions. Such a person may need assistance from a number of mental health, education, and human development professionals in order to learn appropriate ways of expressing anger.

Keep in mind that, with very few exceptions, even a person who has a mental disorder can choose to change. That choice involves accepting that one has a serious mental health problem, choosing to seek help for that problem from a health professional, and consistently working with the health professional to treat the problem.

Reflection Questions

1. Bring to mind at least three situations in which you have lost your temper. Which types of self-talk described in this chapter seem to "fit" with the self-talk that led to losing your temper in each situation?

2. Think about the areas of your life in which you are asked to accept responsibility. Describe these situations to a trusted friend or family member. How do you show responsibility in those activities? What would happen if you behaved irresponsibly?

3. In your own words, describe why losing your temper would be considered irresponsible?

4. How has losing your temper interfered with others' rights in the past?

Chapter 4
Managing Anger in the Moment

One has to start somewhere in order to learn to manage anger successfully. People who want to control their anger must first learn to identify and respond appropriately to anger each time it occurs. Short-term anger management requires a set of techniques to control responses to anger and avoid responding aggressively. In this chapter, you will learn a process to accomplish the following objectives:

- *identify the cues that you are becoming angry;*

- *identify your angry attitudes and angry self-talk;*

- *decide how you will talk to yourself to control your anger; and*

- *take actions that your anger in way that are not aggressive.*

SWaTAT: *A Short-term Anger Management Technique*

The anger management technique described here includes nine steps. The first four steps are preliminary ones. In these steps, you learn what you do when you are angry and create new thoughts and behaviors to enable you to manage your anger. The remaining five steps of the process are the action steps. They enable you to actually stop your angry self-talk before you lose control, and apply your new thinking and behavior in a situation where you have become angry. The action steps are called *SWaTAT* (Stop, Walk, Think, Access, Talk). The *preliminary* steps are as follows:

Step 1:   **Learning Your Physical Anger Cues**

Step 2:   **Identifying Your Angry Attitudes, Self-Talk, and Behaviors**

Step 3:   **Creating New Self-Talk and Behavior**

Step 4:   **Deciding to Act**

The SWaTAT *action* steps, used in a situation where you are becoming angry, are as follows:

Step 5: *S***top What You Are Doing and Saying**

Step 6: *Wa***lk Away From the Situation**

Step 7: *T***hink About What To Do**

Step 8: *A***ccess a Friend**

Step 9: *T***alk It Out**

Step 1: Identify the physical cues that you are angry.

What kinds of physical feelings (e.g., tightness in chest, lump in throat, hot flashes) do you feel as you become angry? How do those sensations change as you get angrier and as you get uncontrollably angry? Over the next few days, pay attention to those feelings and write them down. Be specific when writing down the feelings. You will use them as cues that you're becoming angry, to know when to go to the next step in the program.

Step 2: Determine what you are telling yourself that is making you uncontrollably angry in situations where you lose control.

Identify your thinking that leads you to lose control when you are angry. Bring to mind one or two recent (within the past two weeks) situations where you exhibited poor management of your anger. Write them down. Again, be very specific when describing he feeling.

Remember exactly you did after you had the angry self-talk you recalled above. Ideally, your description of what you did should specific enough that readers could see you do it in their imaginations!

Step 3: Think of other thoughts that would not have led to such anger in those situations.

Now think about what you could have said to yourself instead, that would have led to your remaining in control in each of those situations. These alternate thoughts cast the situation about which you were angry, in a more positive way. Write down your specific alternate thoughts.

Now, think of the action or actions you would take if you told yourself the things you have written above, rather than what you usually tell yourself. Write them down.

Step 4: Respond to the following question: Would you be willing to "force" yourself to think these new thoughts and use the new behaviors the next time you're angry at something or someone?

YES   NO

If your answer is "yes," then write each new thoughts and behaviors on a 4 X 6 index card as soon as possible. Keep the card in your pocket, wallet, or other convenient place at all times. Refer to it at least *five times* throughout the day between rising and retiring, whether you are angry or not, but at least three times when you are not angry. *If your answer was "no," you may stop reading here -- these steps will not work for you.*

Use the following steps the next time you are angry.

Step 5: STOP what you are doing and saying.

Simply stop. *Make no excuses not to stop.* If necessary, keep a rubber band on your wrist and snap it when you feel the physical sensations that let you know you're getting angry enough to lose control. Others, if they and you wish, can help you stop by providing you with a *cue word*, that is, a word or phrase (e.g., "you're losing it") that will remind you to stop. Later in this chapter, I will describe the features of a good cue and give examples of how you and your support person can use cues to help you start this anger management process.

Step 6: (Walk) Turn and Leave.

Simply turn around without another word and leave the scene. You'll come back later to work things out. Others in this situation should know why you're leaving and allow you to do so.

Step 7: Think While You Walk.

Walk for at least 10 minutes. Do a slow burn, cuss under your breath, whatever. But walk it off. As you walk, read the alternate thoughts you wrote on the index card in your pocket. *It is in your pocket, isn't it?*

Step 8: (Access) Call or Visit Your Designated Friend.

Have in mind a friend who will talk with you during times when you are angry. After 10 minutes, go to a phone and call that friend. Talk to this person for a minimum of five minutes about anything the two of you wish. Remember, no drinking or drugs during this time!

Step 9: Talk It Out.

When you think you are ready, return to the scene of your anger and try working things out, using your alternate thoughts about the situation (See Step 3). However, if you do not think you are calm enough to return and work things out, continue to walk and ponder your alternate thoughts for at least 10 more minutes. Remember that, if you have a support person, that person may "send you off" for an additional "cooling off" period if you are not sufficiently calm.

SWaTAT Example: Case of Tom

To illustrate the use of the SWaTAT model, let us use the case of Tom. For much of his adult life, Tom had been a very angry, hostile person. His anger outbursts had led to several job terminations, a few fistfights, and two convictions for intimidation. He had lost nearly all of his friends. His neighbors, as well as his wife, were afraid of him.

As part of his probation agreement following the conviction for intimidation, Tom was ordered to receive anger management counseling. Although he was hostile at first to the idea of counseling, he soon had a good relationship with his counselor and decided that it was good time to make a change in his life before his emotions led to a tragic outcome. The following paragraphs present his thoughts, feelings, and actions as he progressed through the preliminary steps of the SWaTAT model.

Step 1: Identify the physical cues that you are angry.

Tom realized that, as he got angrier, he could feel a "lump" in his stomach, pressure like a tightening band in his chest, and dryness in his throat. He also realized that, in the seconds before he began to scream or pound with his fists, he could feel the beginning of a headache just in front of both temples.

Step 2: Determine what you are telling yourself that is making you uncontrollably angry in situations where you lose control.

At first, Tom had trouble bringing to mind what he "said in his head" during the period leading up to his "anger meltdowns," as he called them. Over a period of several days, he thought about specific situations during which he had become uncontrollably angry and worked hard to recall what he had said to himself in his mind. Finally, he came up with three statements he seemed to say in each situation. They were as follows: (1) "You're stupid! Anyone who thinks that is stupid! Stupid pisses me off!" (2) "Think like me!" And (3) "Any time someone argues with me, they're in my face. A *man* doesn't let anybody get in his face! I must fight back!"

After thinking some more, Tom realized that these thoughts made him scream and, in at least one situation, push the person with whom he was quarreling.

Step 3: Think of other thoughts that would not have led to such anger in those situations.

Tom came up with the following alternate thought to help him maintain control of his anger: "I'm not the master of the universe.

Everyone's entitled to his own ideas. My take on things is no better or worse than anyone else's take on things." Tom decided that, if he acted honestly on this thought, then he would listen carefully to the other person's statements and try to either reason with the person or "cut a deal" so both the other person and he would get something they wanted from the dispute.

Step 4: Respond to the following question: Would you be willing to "force" yourself to think these new thoughts and use the new behaviors the next time you're angry at something or someone?

Although the answer requires only a simple "yes" or "no," Tom spent two days thinking about the extent to which he was willing to commit himself to this process of controlling his anger. He decided that the benefits of managing his anger more successfully were well worth the effort and, sometimes, the discomfort and frustration that his commitment to the procedure would require of him.

Tom selected a long time friend as his access person for Step 8 in the action part of the model. He contacted his friend, who eagerly agreed to assist Tom by talking to him as he was walking off his anger. Tom also showed the anger management steps to his wife, who agreed to support him by reminding him to use Step 6 (Stop) when his anger was becoming uncontrollable, and indicating through a mutually agreeable signal that he should use Step 6 (Walk away). The couple agreed that, when she believed Tom's anger had become greater than he could control, she would state calmly but firmly, "Tom, stop it, you're getting too angry. Use the tools your counselor gave you!"

When Tom stopped speaking, his spouse would say, "Tom, one of your tools is to leave for awhile until you calm down, and call your friend while you're away." In later counseling sessions, Tom recalled that these cues helped him recognize when he was getting too angry and start using the anger management plan's action steps.

Tips for Support Persons

When you help an angry person who is using the steps above, you have an important part in that person's success. You will cue the angry person to begin the anger management process, encourage the person to complete the process, provide a means for that person to leave the anger-producing situation, and assist the person in discussing that situation more calmly when the anger has subsided. Ideally, you are willing to be a support person. The angry person may not succeed in managing his or her anger without the support you can provide. If you are not willing to provide the support, you may choose to allow someone else to be the support person. However, this may be difficult if the angry person is your spouse or someone with whom you live. In the rest of this chapter, I will describe the support person's tasks.

First, you are the one who provides the cue to the angry person, the word, phrase or action that reminds the person to begin Step 4 of the anger management process. In the heat of the moment, the angry person is likely to forget to manage anger or, frankly, may be too carried away by anger to remember to manage it. *Provide the cue exactly as you and the angry person have agreed that it should be provided.* Do not change or elaborate on the cue, as the angry person must receive it exactly as it was practiced.

Second, you help the angry person work through Step 6 of the anger management process, leaving the situation. Unless you have a compelling reason (e.g., the person has threatened to harm self or someone else) to keep the angry person from leaving, you should allow the person leave and, in fact, insist on it. This may be difficult for you to do. In anger-charged conflicts, you may be as angry as the person you are trying to support! You may want the person to stay and argue it out with you.

It is very important that you allow the person to leave. Remember, if the conflict has reached the point that you had to cue the angry person to use this anger management process, *there is no more to be accomplished at that time.* You have nothing to gain by continuing the conflict. Tempers must cool and they must cool *now*, before something unfortunate happens. Let the angry person leave. If the angry person will not leave after you provide the cue, remind the person that Step 6 requires it. If the angry person still will not leave, then *you* must have a place where you can go in order to leave the situation. Leave and go to that place immediately. In no case should you allow the conflict to continue.

Third, you can support the angry person by helping that person use Step 9, talking out the conflict calmly. Once the angry person returns, determine that the person has actually calmed down. If the person hasn't calmed down or has not calmed down sufficiently, ask them to continue Step 6 for another 10 minutes. If the person has calmed down enough to talk reasonably, resume your conversation, encouraging the angry person to use alternate thoughts about the situation that he has created. As you talk, both of you will replace anger-provoking statements and questions with conflict resolution communication, such as behavioral feedback. These communication techniques will be discussed in the next chapter.

Reflection Questions

1. As you have been learning this anger management technique, discuss with your support person (or another trusted friend or family member) the difficulties you have encountered when putting the steps into practice. Which steps are hardest to use and why?

2. What can you do to make it easier to use each step in this anger management technique?

3. Reflect on your experience in using this technique to manage your anger thus far. What have your efforts at anger management showed you about who you are, that is, your beliefs. attitudes, and values?

4. Which of your beliefs, attitudes, or values have helped you learn and use these anger management techniques? Which attitudes, beliefs, and values have hindered your efforts to use the techniques successfully?

Chapter 5
The Selfless Lifestyle

Although the anger management techniques described in Chapter 4 are helpful in situations when you are either becoming angry or already angry, the goal of this book is not simply for you to manage your anger each time it flares up. An equally important goal is that you will recognize the situations in which you most frequently become angry, identify the self-talk that results in your anger, and become skilled at managing your anger before it becomes out of your control. This chapter will describe the importance of reviewing and changing one's attitudes and beliefs in order to develop the quality of *selflessness*, which is essential to effective anger management. The rest of this book will present several techniques for permanently changing angry thoughts and behaviors and creating a selfless lifestyle. As you will learn, these techniques are actually ways to change your thought processes and lifestyle so you can approach situations in your daily life more calmly, without need to be hostile.

This process may take weeks or months to complete and you must use this process to work on changing your beliefs *even at times when you not angry*. In fact, making any changes in your beliefs or any other aspect of your character is easier when you are not angry.

Get Over Yourself! Selflessness

In a famous passage from the Bible, Jesus was in the Garden of Olives awaiting those soldiers to whom Judas had betrayed him. Knowing the suffering he was soon to endure, Jesus asked his Father to allow him to avoid crucifixion. But, after asking to be spared his torture and death, Jesus then made a profound statement, saying, "But if this cup cannot pass from me, *then Thy will and not my will be done.*

Whether or not one is a Christian, or even religious, is not important (actually, a passage of this type is found in the primary texts of almost all religions and spiritual traditions). The meaning of this story for daily life is clear. When we focus excessively on what we want, on our needs and desires, we often fail to take others' viewpoints and needs into account, and we become indignant when we do not get our way. *We must get over ourselves and put others' needs before our own.*

It is sometimes very difficult to set aside what we want or what we think is important, to the wishes or needs of others. But, we must face the truth that our anger at others often is the result of our selfish belief that *our way must prevail*. In most cases when we believe our ways of understanding or doing something is the way it must be, we are simply being stubborn. We need to get over ourselves! The ability to understand, respect, and try out others' viewpoints on situations and problems, is known as *selflessness.*

Features of a Selfless Lifestyle

Selflessness is the product of several attitudes and personal characteristics. When people adopt these attitudes and characteristics, they find that anger ceases to be a significant part of their daily lives. Features of a selfless lifestyle are described below.

Immediacy

Immediacy is one's willingness to form values and attitudes about the world and other people based on their experiences in the here and now, that is, at the current time in one's life rather than hurtful experiences in the past. An immediate person can let go of past hurts and relate to people based on how those people act in the present, not how the person was treated by others in the past. In the next chapter, I will describe in detail how a person who has been hurt in the past can let go of the hurt, in order to let go of the anger that accompanies the hurt and hinders the person's relationships in the present.

Empathy

Empathy is ability to understand another's person's feelings, needs, and actions. Empathy has been called the ability to "walk a mile in another's shoes" and understand why they feel as they do about a situation. One does not have to actually feel the other person's emotion in order to have empathy for the other. One simply has to understand the other's feeling and accept the other's goals and needs in a conflict.

Most people have the ability to be empathic, but must work to bring out this quality in themselves. For some people, it is a particularly difficult trait to develop. People who are often angry or become intensely angry usually have had problems developing their empathic skill. Many people must practice diligently by making conscious efforts to behave empathically. Once developed, however, empathic behavior becomes quite natural.

Respect

Selfless people respect others' needs. They value others as equal to themselves and accept others' ideas as being as worthwhile as their own ideas. They are willing to negotiate with others so that everyone's goals can be achieved. They are able to give and take when working with others to solve problems and do consider the only solution to be "my way or the highway."

Trust

Trust is an essential part of selflessness. If I cannot trust others, then I will approach relationships with the mindset that the other will, by human nature, cheat, lie to, put me down, backstab, or otherwise get the better of me unless I prevent it. Because I resent being cheated, lied to, and the like, I will be looking for a fight in all of my relationships. I will mistrust everyone from the cashier who is giving me my change to my own family members. From a psychologist's point of view, mistrust is always connected with some level of hostility. The more one mistrusts another, the greater the hostility the one may feel.

Generally, there are two reasons that people do not trust. One reason is that they have been hurt by others in whom they placed their trust, and have decided that they will never allow themselves to be hurt again. The second reason is that they were never taught as children to trust others, and were raised in families where the adults did not display trust. Since one cannot do what one has not learned, these persons have never known trust for others.

Trust is not learned easily. In order to trust, people must do the very thing they probably don't want to do -- believe in someone and find out what happens. But, when untrusting people risk trust and find that others are trustworthy, they gradually learn to take the risk more often until they become trusting people.

Confidence

In order to be selfless, one must have confidence. When a people have confidence in themselves and their ideas, they do not feel pressure to defend their ideas or put down others in order in order to feel good about themselves. Confident people seldom feel threatened by others . They accept others as equals and do not react aggressively when others challenge their ideas or express different ideas. Confident people are not afraid to negotiate solutions to conflicts because they are comfortable with themselves and the validity of their beliefs.

Responsibility

Selfless people take responsibility, that is, they hold themselves accountable, for their behavior. They accept that they are in control of what they feel, think, say, and do at all times. When they make an error, or behave poorly, they accept the consequences of their actions. They avoid blaming other people or circumstances for their behavior. Nor do they accept membership In the *I Can't Club*, by complaining that they aren't capable of behaving differently. They avoid manipulating others with their statements and behavior.

Humility

Selfless people are humble. Although they express their ideas and needs clearly and confidently, they consider others as their equals.

When appropriate, they place others' needs and ideas before, or on the same level as, their own needs and ideas.

Humility, like trust, is a particularly difficult characteristic for some people to fully develop. It often requires a person to not only accept confrontation by others when the person behaves in a self-centered way, but also to seek out that confrontation from others. Others who function as support persons must be able and willing to kindly confront a self-centered person in order to bring self-centeredness to that person's attention.

Patience

In many ways, we live in an instant outcome world. Many people have come to expect things to always happen quickly in their lives. We eat fast food, seek medical care from 15 minute urgent clinics, obtain 60 second responses to our credit applications, and use instant messaging with friends and co-workers. When one becomes accustomed to such instant gratification, one may become impatient and angry when one is required to wait.

Our world often does not encourage patience, but it is a trait necessary for selfless living and for good anger control. The ability to wait for an outcome allows us to take time to think through problems rather than simply react with anger. Not only are people able to control strong emotions more easily, but they experience fewer medical and mental health problems generally.

Humor

Selfless people do not take themselves too seriously. They understand that most problems in daily life, while important at during the moments when they occur, will not be important or particularly life-altering after those moments have passed. As one of my colleagues often remarks, "In 100 years, no one will know that this situation occurred."

With this attitude, selfless people can, laugh about the situations in which find themselves. They appreciate and enjoy the humor in many routine situations. They accept their own peculiarities and those of others without being threatened or offended by those peculiarities. Quite simply, it is fun to be with them.

Selfless Attitudes and Self-Talk

In Chapter 2, you learned about several other kinds of self-talk that caused people to become angry. At this point, it's time to review those beliefs and think about what kind of beliefs fit with a less angry, selfless lifestyle. Each angry belief in Chapter 2 will be presented again below, followed by an example of an alternate, selfless belief written as a self-statement. After you read the example of the selfless belief, you should write down another alternate selfless belief in your own words, that reflects your own situation. In Appendix B, there is a form to help you with this activity. The form lists each angry belief in Chapter 2, the alternate belief discussed in this chapter, and blank lines to allow you to state an alternate belief in your own words.

1. *"I find your behavior directly threatening to me in some way and must react aggressively to stop the threat."*

Psychologists have found that people who live selfless lives are willing to trust others. People who trust others tend not to find others' actions personally threatening. When you believe that, as a general rule, people are not "out to get you," then you are unlikely to feel a need to become intensely angry or react defensively toward others.

Thus, a selfless alternative belief would allow you to tell yourself that others are not threatening you, nor are they out to get you. An example of such a self-statement would be as follows:

"People are not out to get me. I disagree with what this person does (or says), but I can work with the person to solve the problem."

Now, write a similar self-statement in your own words.

2. *"I believe that you are cheating or taking advantage of me, and I must fight back to protect my rights."*

Again, unwillingness to trust others is the force behind this anger-producing belief. A selfless alternative belief would remind you that the other person is probably not cheating you, but asserting that person's own needs. Even if this person is cheating you, you can protect your rights without being angry about it. Thus, an alternate self-statement might be as follows:

" People are not out to get me. I'm probably not being cheated and, even if I am, it's not such a big deal. I can cope with it."

Now, write a similar self-statement in your own words.

3. *"My authority is being challenged and this must not happen."*

Two characteristics of a selfless lifestyle will help you overcome this kind of self-talk. Those characteristics are *humility* and *patience*. Humility is the ability to allow others to share control of situations with you. Psychologists often write about the problems experienced by persons with so-called "high control needs." Whether or not we control the show is usually not the issue in a conflict. The important issue is that others get what they need, or are protected, in a situation. Many people need to accept that they don't need to the full control or authority of a situation in order to be worthwhile, effective people.

Patience enables people to take their time, and allow others to take their time, when working through a problem or resolving a conflict. Impatient people are often angry and their anger is often intense. If you expect tasks to be performed quickly, according to a rigid schedule, you are likely to easily become angry if those tasks are done as quickly as you expected.

Thus, new self-statements might be along the following lines:

"I don't need to be seen as the Big Boss; I need to work this conflict out so we both get what we need," or

"Slow down, have patience."

Now, write a similar self-statement in your own words.

4. *"In some way, I am failing or" not getting the job done."*

This self-statement emphasizes the importance of confidence in a selfless lifestyle. The important point of an alternative self-statement is to reassure yourself that you're not failing and, even if you were not succeeding, you are going to get it right. Thus, an alternate statement might be as follows:

"I've not failed. I can do this well."

Now, write a self-statement in your own words.

5. *"I'm better than everyone else; no one can tell me what to do or how things should be. I want what I want, period!"*

The type of alternative statement in this case is clear and simple.

"Thy needs, not my needs, be always done."

Now, write a self-statement in your own words.

6. *"Anytime someone challenges you (or disagrees with you, or gets in your face), you better take care of it by fighting (yelling, breaking something)."*

Alternative self-statements may take several forms. For example, you may need to revise your beliefs about what your sex (i.e., male or female) is supposed to do in conflicts. Or you may simply need to change your belief to one in which aggression is not an acceptable way to solve a problem. An example of such an alternative self-statement is as follows:

"I will work out conflicts by listening and compromising. Aggression is never an acceptable substitute."

Or, another possible self-statement might be as follows:

"A man (woman, boy, girl) solves problems by talking it through, not fighting."

Now, write a similar self-statement in your own words.

7. *"I can't control myself. My anger just happens all of a sudden and I do something aggressive before I realize it!"*

The alternative self-statement is based on a simple principle that you must accept. You *can* control yourself. It's time to resign your membership in the *I Can't Club* and assume responsibility for your feelings, thoughts, and actions. Thus, an example of selfless alternative self-statement would be as follows:

"In all situations, at all times, I can control my emotions and actions."

Now, write a similar self-statement in your own words.

Reflection Questions

1. In this chapter, the selfless lifestyle is descried in terms of several characteristics. How much of those characteristics do you have at this time? Which characteristics, if any, would you consider strengths? Which ones, if any, would you consider weaknesses?

2. After you have answered the above yourself, ask a trusted friend or family member to respond to it based on what that person knows about you. How are your impressions about yourself similar to, and different from, the impressions of this person?

3. Which of the selfless characteristics do you think will be hardest for you to learn and display consistently? Why? How can you make it easier to learn those characteristics?

Chapter 6
Long-Term Anger Management

This chapter will describe additional techniques for avoiding unproductive anger. They are intended to be practiced regularly, whether or not one has felt angry, as part of one's lifestyle. Commit to all these techniques in your lifestyle, beginning today.

Letting Go: Getting Over the Past

Many of our beliefs about the world and other people come about from our past experiences, especially our experiences as children and teens. If people have warm, satisfying, and kind experiences with others while growing up, they usually enter adulthood with good, hopeful beliefs about the world, themselves, and others around them. On the other hand, people who have harsh, unpleasant, or abusive experiences with others as they grew up may enter adulthood with hostile, suspicious, and hopeless beliefs.

Thus, people who have angry worldviews often have been hurt physically or emotionally as children. They are wounded by actions, real and imagined, that were, or seemed at the time, harsh, neglectful, or cruel from people they may have trusted or from strangers over whom they had no power to fight. In adulthood, these people continue evaluate others as threatening and are always prepared to fight back, *even though there is no longer anything to fight about.*

Most people who are angry about something in the past are reasonable enough to know that they should not stay angry about what they cannot change. Their minds tell them that they should not have beliefs and attitudes now, based on things that happened to them in the past. But, their hearts do not allow them let go of the hurt. As one patient told me, "I know I should let it go, Dad's dead and he no longer abuses me. But I can't. I just can't get over my anger and hatred of him."

There is no magic formula for letting go. If you are angry about hurts from the past, you must convince yourself to let go of those hurts each time you realize your anger is related to those hurts. , You can form new thoughts about others that will free you from your anger only when you have let go of past hurts.

It is common for people who have been hurt to want to know *why* they were hurt. Perhaps they were abused, abandoned, treated cruelly, were involved in a traumatic event, or denied an important opportunity. Whatever the hurt, the question that often holds a person back from letting the hurt go is, "Why did he (she) do this to me?"

Although you may believe intensely and sincerely that it is important, the question of why something bad happened in a person's life is almost never relevant to letting go of the hurt. Asking why is irrelevant for two reasons.

First, there seldom is an answer. Most often the honest answer to the question, "Why did this happen to me?" is simply, "It just did. You were in the place and time for it to happen." Similarly, the answer to the question, "Why did he (or she) do those things to me?" is, "He (or she) simply felt like it at the time." *There is no other reason.*

Second, if there were an answer, it would not help in letting go of the hurt. For most people, *asking* "why" is simply a way of *saying*, "How could you? I'm so angry at you! Take back the hurt! Make it go away!" Of course, this can never happen. Once someone hurts you, that person cannot undo the hurt. The person may seek your forgiveness. You can choose to forgive or simply choose to set aside the hurt and not let it influence you in the future. So, you see that asking why actually holds you back from letting go. Instead, decide that the bad things in life happen "just because."

Some hurts are, in any reasonable person's opinion, terrible -- physical abuse, severe neglect, sexual molestation, and other kinds of trauma. It is very hard, perhaps impossible, to forgive the person who caused the hurt. However, it is not always necessary to forgive a person who hurt you, in order to let go of the hurt. A technique I often use with my patients is called *dropping the charges.* It is based on the common practice in court cases when the judge decides that, after hearing the evidence, decides the case should not be pursued further and dismisses it. The defendant often is not determined to be guilty or innocent of the charge or, in some cases, it may have been established that the defendant committed the offense. The charges against the defendant are simply set aside for other reasons.

Dropping the charges against someone who hurt you in the past is the same type of action. The person who hurt you remains guilty of the "crime" and you may not forgive the person. You make a conscious decision to set aside the hurt so that the offense will no longer influence your thoughts, feelings, and behavior in the future. Dropping the charges has four steps. These steps are described below.

Step 1: State the hurt clearly. In order to set aside a hurt, you must be able to state it to yourself. I believe that the best way to clarify your hurt is to write it down. Write it as clearly as you can, then say it out loud to yourself.

Step 2: Decide how the hurt has affected you in the present. How has the hurt, and your anger about that hurt, shaped your attitudes and beliefs? In particular, how has the hurt shaped your angry thoughts and beliefs? If you could let go of the hurt, how would your angry beliefs change? How would act differently if your angry beliefs changed?

Step 3: Express your anger. Say out loud that you angry about the hurt. This may seem silly at first, since you've probably known you were angry about this hurt for a long time. Nonetheless, say out loud that you angry about it now. If it helps, shout or scream your anger. Ask why the person hurt you. Demand vengeance. Say whatever comes to mind.

After venting your anger alone or with a trusted companion, you may find it helpful to obtain a photograph of the person who hurt you, and speak directly at the photograph. As you gaze at the photograph, bring that person into the room with you. Tell the person exactly how you feel about the hurt and about him or her, as if this person were there and willing to listen to you without interrupting you. You may wish to write out exactly what you say to the person prior to conducting this activity, so you will not forget what you want to say. Again, shout at the person if you wish. Tell the person what you think or him or her. You should dialogue with the picture for no more than five minutes at a time. But, you may engage in the dialogue as many times as you need to vent all of your anger. You may find it important to have a trusted companion with you while you dialogue with the person in the photograph, because the conversation may bring about very intense emotions.

Step 4: Drop the charges. After you have vented completely, say out loud these or similar words, "I will not forgive you for choosing to do what you did to me. But I will not allow what you did to keep holding me back. I drop my anger against you. From now on, I will consider you insane and will not give you or this matter further weight in my life."

You probably will find that you need to repeat these statements several times, on more than one occasion, in order to completely believe them and truly drop the anger against the person who committed the hurt. Also, remember that you must be committed to dropping the anger. Be mindful of the fact that many people who are angry at someone in the past, hold onto their anger because in some they benefit from their anger. It may seem absurd, but many people actually are comforted by their resentments toward others. Some people use their anger about past hurts as an excuse to behave badly in the present (e.g., an alcoholic in court for his fourth DWI charge tells the judge, "I get drunk in order to forget how I was abused by my father. I can't get over it, so I can't stop drinking!"). Others may use hurts to get revenge on the people who hurt them by repeatedly inducing guilt in those people. The induction of the guilt feels good even though it does not relieve the anger. Unless you think honestly about how your anger may serve you, you cannot let the anger.

Step 5: Commit to new beliefs and behavior. Recall from Step 2 the way your beliefs would change if you let go of your anger. Now, make a commitment to using those beliefs and the behaviors that go along with those beliefs.

This technique, while straightforward, requires considerable effort to complete successfully. However, living in the present and letting go of the past is a necessary part of the selfless lifestyle. With commitment, practice, and the support of those who are close to you, it is possible to let go and "forget without forgiving."

The Affirmation Ritual

After you have reviewed your angry beliefs while working through Chapter 5, you probably will identify several beliefs you will need to change. One way to accomplish an enduring change in your beliefs is through a daily *affirmation ritual*. An affirmation ritual is an activity, usually performed when one first rises in the morning, in which a person reads and reflects upon the beliefs by which one wishes to live life that day. By reviewing these beliefs each, one not only memorizes them, but keeps them fresh in mind and renews a commitment to living according to them.

In order to prepare for an affirmation ritual, follow these steps:

Step 1: List your non-angry beliefs. Remember when you listed the beliefs and attitudes that allowed you to become angry, then replaced those beliefs and attitudes with beliefs that allowed you to manage in situations without losing control? Those "non-angry" beliefs and attitudes will form the core of the affirmations you will you review each morning. You can find additional affirmations in inspiration books as well as booklets containing affirmations, proverbs, and inspirational sayings.

If you not done so already, print each of those beliefs on separate three by five inch, or four by six inch, index cards. Next, think about other beliefs and attitudes that would allow you to manage situations positively without becoming uncontrollably or inappropriately angry. Write each of those beliefs on separate index cards as well.

As a general rule, five to ten affirmation cards is a good number with which to start. Over time, you should add additional affirmations when you find a new belief non-angry or otherwise positive living that inspires you. From the outset, however, the first two affirmations in your list should be as follows: (1) *I will be a selfless, not selfish, person*, and (2) *Thy will, not my will, be always done.*

Step 2: Create a card file or booklet. Place all of your affirmation cards in a card file or punch holes in them and use binder rings (available at most discount or office supply stores) to form them into a booklet.

Step 3: Review the affirmations daily. Every morning, after you rise and complete your "morning routine," read your affirmations in a quiet, comfortable place. Read each affirmation to yourself, then silently answer each of the following questions: (1) What does this affirmation mean to me today? (2) How will I live this affirmation today? (3) What obstacle or obstacles may hold me back from living this affirmation today? (4) How can I prevent this obstacle (or these obstacles) from occurring?

Your review of your affirmations should take at least 30 minutes. As you add more affirmations, the time you set aside for your review should increase also. Generally, my patients who have reviewed their affirmations for several years set aside an hour to an hour and one-quarter for this activity each morning. It is important that you make this morning are view a priority every day; do not put it off or cancel it when you are busy. Make it happen regardless of other commitments. Although this review can be performed prior to going to bed at night, I have found that it is best performed first thing in the morning.

Deferral

The ability to place another's needs and ideas before one's own is an important defining feature of selflessness. I call this skill *deferral*. It requires a combination of empathy, respect, confidence, patience, and even humor. Each time you defer to someone else's goal or point of view in a disagreement, you take a positive step toward developing those characteristics in yourself.

Beginning today and for the next month, commit to a change in your attitude about others around you. Specifically, the new attitude is as follows:

"When I disagree with someone, I will make a point to understand what the other person wants, then defer what I want in favor of what the other person wants."

For the next month, each time you disagree with someone on any matter, you will defer to that person's wishes instead of your own (unless doing so would truly jeopardize you or someone else, as would be the case if you agreed to do something illegal). On one hand, you will almost certainly find this difficult to do at first. On the hand, you may come to notice that deferring your wishes and needs to others' also is rather freeing. Your goal should be that, after a month, your ability to understand and value the viewpoints of others becomes increasingly easier. As your empathy improves, you also will find it easier to understand the reasons others have goals and needs that differ from your own, and be more willing to accommodate those differences without becoming angry about it.

Action Delay Technique

Beginning right now, make a commitment to yourself that, regardless hat happens to you during the course of daily life, no matter how you initially about what someone does or what they say that you may not like, you will not react right at that moment. Instead, decide that, as an attitude change, you will wait at least *30 minutes* before responding to others' actions or statements that initially make you angry. Write this commitment down in your affirmation file or this book. Review it every morning before you engage the first task of your day. If, during the day, you slip and react with anger before stopping to reflect on the situation, recommit yourself to the policy at the end of the day and review it again the next day.

Humor

As discussed in Chapter 5, an important part of leaving an angry lifestyle behind involves not taking oneself too seriously. It is useful to be able to laugh at one's mistakes and see the bright side of situations that, on the surface, appear bad. Beginning today, set for yourself the goal that you will find at least one situation each day at which you can laugh. You will soon find that, as you approach problems with an eye for the humor in those situations, you will actually find that some situations you used to take so seriously, are now rather humorous and even insignificant.

Anger Journal

As part of their anger management therapy, I ask my patients to keep an anger journal. The journal, usually kept in a small notebook with lined paper, enables persons to track and analyze situations during which they became angry, and explore better ways to act in those situations.

To keep an anger journal, obtain a school notebook (available at discount and office supply stores). When you encounter a situation during which you became angry, describe it in your journal as soon as possible after the situation occurs. The entry should include the following information:

1. What happened in the situation?
2. What did you feel that let you know you were getting angry?
3. What did you tell yourself as you became angry?
4. What did you do?
5. If you managed your anger successfully, how did you accomplish this? How do you feel with your success?
6. If you did not manage your anger successfully, how did you feel after the situation ended? What could you say to yourself differently if the situation happened again? What could you do differently?
7. What obstacles could hinder you from thinking and acting as you proposed in Step 6? How can you prevent those obstacles?

As you keep your journal over time, the new beliefs you create while performing Step 6 above, can be added to your box or booklet of affirmations that you review each morning.

Use Feedback

What people say and how they talk to one another during a conflict will determine if the conflict is resolved or escalates to an emotional boiling point. In my work with persons in conflict (most of the time, these are couples or families), I have found that persons must use specific communication rules in order to have a *quarrel*, that is, a conflict during which persons' anger escalates to the point where they feel out of control and the conflict cannot be resolved. Some of these rules are as follows:

1. Raise your voice. Scream, shout or, at least, talk very loudly.

2. Use profanity liberally.

3. Insult the other person. Call that person names, the uglier the name, the better.

4. Insult the other person further by making *character attacks*. To make a character attack, simply accuse the other person of having a personality flaw, then accuse the person of causing an undesired situation to exist because of the flaw. For example, a wife uses a character attack against her husband when she tells him, "If you were a real man instead of a wimp, your son wouldn't be in trouble at school!" Insult the other person as much as possible through these attacks.

5. Explain your reason for your point of view in the quarrel in as much detail as possible. Be very, very specific and opinionated. Defend your position fiercely. Under no circumstances act like you heard or care about the other person's point of view.

6. If you cannot refute the other person's point of view, confuse the other person by getting off the subject. Even better, use a character attack to insult the person by stating that the person has this opinion because of stupidity or a similar bad personal trait.

7. Violate the other person's physical safe space. To do this, stand very close to the other person, preferably in a way that prevents the person from moving away from you or leaving the situation. Even more effective, poke, touch, or strike the person.

8. If the other person touches, pokes, or strikes you, become very hysterical. Scream, cry, curse, break things, or even run around as if you had lost your mind. This is very good for disorienting the other person.

In productive conflicts, the conflicting people instead use *interpersonal feedback* to express their feelings and needs, and negotiate changes in one another's behavior. If you use interpersonal feedback in a conflict with another person, you choose to tell the other how a specific behavior from that person makes you feel, and requests that person to change the behavior in a particular way that would enable you to feel better. The following example illustrates how a feedback message is communicated.

Jack and Jill are a married couple. Normally, Jack arrives home about 30 minutes after leaving work. During the past three nights, he has come home more than an hour after work. Jill is not really concerned that he was later than usual in arriving home, as he has additional obligations at work from time to time. But, she is angry that he did not call to tell her he was not coming home at the usual time. Because he did not call, she did not know when to plan dinner. Yesterday, she had to abruptly arrange to take their daughter to a practice session that normally was his responsibility. On this evening, when he arrived late, she communicated to him the following feedback message:

"Jack when you don't come home at the usual time and don't call to tell me you'll be late, I feel angry. I want you to call me when you know you're going to be late and let me know what time you'll be home."

Psychologists refer to the message above as a *corrective behavioral feedback statement*. This statement has several important characteristics.

First, the statement has three parts. The first part clearly states the *behavior* that concerns the speaker. It is essential that your feedback point out a behavior rather than attack the feedback recipient (as in, "Jack you're really inconsiderate!"). The second part clearly states the speakers *emotional reaction* to the behavior. In the example above, Jill feels angry (*emotional reaction*) when Jack doesn't call (*behavior of concern to Jill*) to let her know he'll be late. The third part, which is optional, clearly asks for a change in the feedback recipient's behavior (Jill tells Jack she wants him to call when he knows he will be late (*requested behavior change*).

Note that the feedback message does *not* provide a reason for the speaker's feeling when the recipient's behavior occurs. In the example above, Jill does not try to explain why she feels angry when Jack doesn't call when he is going to be late. Nor does the speaker give a reason for the specific behavior change being requested.

Psychological research on human communication has revealed that people become entangled in conflicts over opinions rather than on feelings. Had Jill tried to explain to Jack why she was angry when he didn't call, he may respond by arguing that she "shouldn't feel that way" or blame her for her feelings. This response almost inevitably results in an argument. Likewise, it is pointless to give an explanation as to why she wants him to call, for he is likely to argue that her reasoning is wrong rather than negotiate another behavior when he is going to be late. If someone's behavior affects you positively or negatively, then *how you feel is simply how you feel*. One can argue that your opinions are right or wrong, good or bad, or accurate, or inaccurate. But, one cannot sensibly argue the right or wrong of your feelings. If Jack does not want to Jill to feel angry when he is going to arrive home late, then he will either honor her request to call ahead or, in the alternative, negotiate another behavior that will suit both of them.

Third, the feedback message clearly and specifically states the behavior to changed, the speaker's feeling, and the behavior desired of the feedback recipient. Also, the feeling expressed in the message is, in fact, an emotion rather than a thought. At times, people state a thought when they intend to state a feeling when giving feedback to another person (e.g., "I feel concerned when you come home late"). Feeling words are derived from the four basic emotions: happy, sad, angry, and frightened. When in doubt as to whether or not you're using a feeling word, rely on the basic four!

It is important to remember that, even though you may give corrective feedback to another person, that person may reuse to honor your request for change, and may even choose to deny or ignore your feedback. Nonetheless, by communicating with feedback, you have succeeded in managing your emotions while clearly communicating your reaction to another's behavior and your request for a behavior change. Although you may not get what you want, you have made your point and increased the chance that the other person will negotiate with you a more desirable behavior now or in the future.

Of course, feedback can be positive as well as corrective. It is very useful to give someone positive feedback before giving a corrective feedback message, as in the following example:

"Jack, I know that sometimes, you have to stay late at work, and I feel happy that you work so hard for our family. But I need you to know that feel angry when you don't let me know that you'll be late. I'd like you just to call and let me know when you'll be late getting home from work."

Moreover, it is useful to give others positive feedback as often as possible and, certainly, every time someone does or says something about which you have good feelings. When you freely give positive feedback to those around you, are much more likely to obtain their cooperation when you want them to change!

Reflection Questions

1. Which of the long-term anger management practices appeals to you most? Why does it appeal to you? Which practice appeals to you least and why is this so?

2. Are you able to think abut others' opinions as being as valid as your own? How about other's needs and feelings? Can you think of a time when, by your reaction to them, you communicated to others that their ideas did not really matter to you? If you lived for a month according to the motto, *Thy will and not mine always be done*, how would your daily life be different?

3. If you were to live for a week using the motto, *Thy will and not mine always be done*, what would be the obstacles that might hinder your efforts to defer your ideas or needs to those of others? How can you overcome those obstacles? What would be the rewards of successfully deferring your ideas and needs to those of others for a month?

Chapter 7
Relaxation and Stress Management

Angry people are tense people. When people become angry, their physical tension increases. If they can become calmer again, the anger may not go away but it will be easier to manage. Although there are many ways one can become more relaxed when tense or agitated, psychologists have developed a technique to relax in a very purposeful, complete way. This technique is known as progressive relaxation. After a person has learned the progressive relaxation technique to become calmer, that person can learn another technique, called rapid relaxation to quickly become calmer in anger-producing situations. In this chapter, you will learn how to use both techniques. However, long-term stress management involves more than simply relaxation. It requires a lifestyle in which steps are routinely taken to manage stress. Some helpful stress management lifestyle practices will be described in the last section of this chapter.

Progressive Relaxation Technique

The goal of progressive relaxation is to make your entire body become as relaxed as possible. Many people have forgotten what it feels like to be in a fully relaxed state. The technique described here also is designed to help you teach your body the difference between the tense and relaxed states so you can decide to become relaxed when you wish to do so.

To begin, find a comfortable place to carry out this technique. In my office, I have a large reclining chair with vibrators in the seat, lower back, and upper back areas. The vibrators are controlled by switches in the recliner's right arm. I have my patients recline to an "almost prone" position in order to conduct the technique. However, you can use any comfortable chair or, if you prefer, lie on a bed, couch, or even the floor. If you lie down, use pillows under your head, arms, and knees. Many people find it helpful to play soft music that they find soothing. There are many kinds of music that work quite well to relax. I recommend recorded programs of classical or New Age music set against a background of ocean or forest sounds.

Some people find that, while they are learning to use this progressive relaxation technique, it is helpful to have someone read the following paragraphs to them slowly. In the alternative, you may wish to make an audiotape of the following paragraphs and play the tape along with the music you have selected. Of course, to play both the tape of these instructions and a music program, you will need two playback devices (e.g., a CD player for the music and a cassette tape player to play these instructions that you recorded). Once you find a comfortable position and started the music, follow these instructions:

Close your eyes and keep them closed throughout the procedure. Make your mind as clear as possible. Take your time with this step, until you have dismissed all intrusive thoughts, (e.g., worries, doubts, plans for the rest of the day) from your mind. When you have cleared your mind, imagine a place and time in your life where you have been most happy. This will be your "quiet place." Imagine yourself in this quiet place and let it completely absorb you. Let yourself be fully in this place and time. If any other thought intrudes, dismiss it. Sweep it completely from your mind and focus on the time and place to which you have taken yourself.

As you enter your quiet place, begin to *body breathe*. That is, *slowly* draw a breath as deeply into your body as you can, as if the leading edge of your breath goes so far inside you that it touches your stomach. It should take two or three seconds to draw the breath all the way into yourself. Hold the breath for three seconds then slowly let it al the way out. As you slowly exhale this breath, imagine that any tension inside you comes out with the breath. Take another slow, deep breath. Imagine that quiet and relaxation enters your body with that breath. Hold that breath three seconds. Now, let it out slowly, all the way out. Again, imagine tension is coming out with that breath, to be replaced by peace and relaxation when you draw in the next breath. Keep doing this, breathing in slowly and deeply, holding it three seconds, and exhaling slowly and completely.

While you breathe, remember to stay in your quiet place. Look around this place. See the details of the scene and hear the sounds that you enjoy. You will soon be working with different areas of your body in order to relax them and you will do so while you are in this place.

Now, in your quiet place, pay attention to your neck and your arms, from your fingers to your shoulders. Let's count to three and, on the count of three, make both arms, from fingers to shoulders, as tense and tight as you can. Try to make them so tense that you feel discomfort. Ready? One, two, three tense up! Hold it! Pay attention to this feeling. This is what your arms are like when they are tense. You can compare this feeling to the relaxation you'll feel when you release this tension. On the count of three, release the tension in your arms. Ready. One, two, three, release! Make all the tension flow of out of your arms, like sand flowing quickly from both shoulders, down your arms, into your hands, and through your fingers onto the floor. Remember to keep breathing slowly and deeply. With each breath in, the tension in your arms is replaced with complete, total, utter, relaxation. Compare this feeling to the tension you created in your arms a moment ago. Imagine telling your arms, "This is relaxed. This is the way I want you to feel all the time." Now, keep breathing and enjoy the relaxation in your arms and the wonder of your quiet place.

Now, in your quiet place, pay attention to your upper torso, that is, your chest, and upper back. Let's count to three and, on the count of three, make your chest and upper back as tense and tight as you can. Imagine that there is a balloon next to your heart that has no air in it. On the count of three, imagine that the balloon quickly fills with so much air that it will burst through your chest. You must make your chest and upper back muscles so tense that the inflating balloon cannot burst through you. Ready? One, two three, tense! Feel the balloon filling up. Tense your muscles and hold it inside you. Don't let it burst through! Pay attention to this feeling. This is what your upper body is like when you are tense. You can compare this feeling to the relaxation you'll feel when you release this tension. On the count of three, release the tension. It will be as if the balloon bursts and all the tension flies out of you when it bursts. Ready? One, two, three, release! Make all the tension fly out of your chest.

Remember to keep breathing slowly and deeply. With each breath in, the tension in your upper body is replaced with complete, total, utter, relaxation. Compare this feeling to the tension you created a moment ago. Imagine telling your upper body, "This is relaxed. This is the way I want you to feel all the time." Now, keep breathing and enjoy the relaxation in your arms and upper torso, and the wonder of your quiet place.

Now, in your quiet place, pay attention to your stomach, abdomen, and lower back. Let's count to three and, on the count of three, make your stomach, abdomen, and lower back as tense and tight as you can. Imagine that there is a balloon next to your stomach that has no air in it. On the count of three, imagine that the balloon quickly fills with so much air that it will burst through your abdomen or your lower back. You must make those muscles so tense that the inflating balloon cannot burst through you. Ready? One, two three, tense! Feel the balloon filling up. Tense your muscles and hold it inside you. Don't let it burst through! Pay attention to this feeling. This is what your stomach, abdomen, and lower back are like when you are tense. You can compare this feeling to the relaxation you'll feel when you release this tension. On the count of three, release the tension. It will be as if the balloon bursts and all the tension flies out of you when it bursts. Ready? One, two, three, release! Make all the tension fly out of your stomach, abdomen, and lower back.

Remember to keep breathing slowly and deeply. With each breath in, the tension is replaced with complete, total, utter, relaxation. Compare this feeling to the tension you created a moment ago. Imagine telling your stomach, abdomen, and lower back, "This is relaxed. This is the way I want you to feel all the time." Now, keep breathing, enjoy the relaxation, and enjoy the wonder of your quiet place.

Now, in your quiet place, pay attention to your legs, from just above your feet up to your hips. Let's count to three and, on the count of three, make your legs as tense and tight as you can. Ready? One, two three, tense! Tense your muscles and hold it inside you. Pay attention to this feeling. This is what your legs are like when you are tense. You can compare this feeling to the relaxation you'll feel when you release this tension. On the count of three, release the tension Ready? One, two, three, release! Make all the tension flow out of your legs, as if the tension were sand, flowing down from your hips through your legs and feet, and out through your toes onto the floor.

Remember to keep breathing slowly and deeply. With each breath in, the tension is replaced with complete, total, utter, relaxation. Compare this feeling to the tension you created a moment ago. Imagine telling your legs, "This is relaxed. This is the way I want you to feel all the time." Now, keep breathing, enjoy the relaxation, and enjoy the wonder of your quiet place.

Now, in your quiet place, pay attention to your feet. Let's count to three and, on the count of three, make your feet as tense and tight as you can. Ready? One, two three, tense! Tense your feet and hold it. Curl your toes under the soles of your feet as far as you can. Pay attention to this feeling. This is what your feet are like when you are tense. You can compare this feeling to the relaxation you'll feel when you release this tension. On the count of three, release the tension Ready? One, two, three, release! Make all the tension flow out of your feet, as if the tension were sand, flowing through your toes onto the floor.

Remember to keep breathing slowly and deeply. With each breath in, the tension is replaced with complete, total, utter, relaxation. Compare this feeling to the tension you created a moment ago. Imagine telling your feet, "This is relaxed. This is the way I want you to feel all the time." Now, keep breathing, enjoy the relaxation, and enjoy the wonder of your quiet place.

Now, in your quiet place, pay attention to your entire body. Let's count to three and, on the count of three, make your entire body, from your toes to the top of your head, as tense and tight as you can. Ready? One, two three, tense! Tense your body and hold it. Pay attention to this feeling. This is what your body is like when you are tense. You can compare this feeling to the relaxation you'll feel when you release this tension. On the count of three, release the tension Ready? One, two, three, release! Make all the tension flow out of your body, through your arms and legs and out of your fingers and toes onto the floor, as if the tension were sand, flowing out of you onto the floor. Remember to keep breathing slowly and deeply. With each breath in, the tension is replaced with complete, total, utter, relaxation. Compare this feeling to the tension you created a moment ago.

Imagine telling your body, "This is relaxed. This is the way I want you to feel all the time." Now, keep breathing, enjoy the relaxation, and enjoy the wonder of your quiet place.

Now for the next five minutes, simply enjoy looking moving about in your quiet place. When you are ready to return to the place where are sitting (or lying down), simply count slowly from five to one. With each number counted, you will feel more alert and ore relaxed. The relaxation you feel now will last the rest of this day. Ready? Count slowly, with five seconds between each number. Five, four, three, two, one.

It will take some time to use this relaxation technique well enough to obtain maximum benefit from it. You should expect to practice it at least twice every day. One practice session should begin right after waking in the morning. The second session should begin right after you go to bed in the evening. If you practice twice a day, you probably will master the technique within six weeks. The more you practice the technique, the easier and more effective it becomes.

Once you master the progressive relaxation technique, you are ready to learn a rapid relaxation technique that will enable you to relax yourself in just a few seconds. This quick technique will be useful when you are in a situation where you have become angry and are using the nine anger management steps to work through your anger.

Rapid Relaxation Technique

This technique requires only a few seconds and works well once you are completely taught your body the difference between tension and relaxation. You must first master the progressive relaxation technique described above, in order for the rapid relaxation to be effective.

To use the technique, first close your eyes. Imagine that you have placed your finger in an electrical outlet. If you have ever actually done this (many children do it, albeit only once!), you know that your entire body tenses and becomes rigid. Thus, as you imagine placing your finger in the outlet, tense your entire body until you feel uncomfortable. Hold this tension for a slow five count. On the count of five, imagine that you pulled your finger free of the outlet. All of the tension will simply evaporate, or flow quickly out of you, along with the electrical current. You will feel much more relaxed.

Beyond relaxation: Stress Management

Although progressive relaxation is an excellent technique for relieving stress when it occurs, the most effective long-term stress solution is to avoid stress in the first place. In the following sections, let us consider ways that one can manage stressors in order to live more calmly.

Many people try to do too much in their daily lives. Doing too much in insufficient time creates a host of health, emotional, family, and social problems. Research investigations on stress and health have revealed a number of common, yet serious, problems associated with excessive stress. Those problems include the following;

Psychological problems

Stress is, perhaps, one of the most common causes of psychological problems. People who are under ongoing or excessive stress levels are much more likely to have symptoms of anxiety, depression, mood swings, and uncontrollable anger. Stress is a frequent contributor to alcohol and drug abuse. In fact, some people who are under constant levels of high stress may exhibit more serious disorders, such as thought disturbances, problems remaining in touch with reality, or even suicidal thoughts.

Sexual problems

Stress is a major contributor to sexual problems in men and women. Men under excessive stress may have difficulties with low sexual desire as well as erectile dysfunction. Women under too much stress often have problems with low sexual desire, discomfort during intercourse, and difficulties having orgasm during sexual relations.

Relationship problems

Stress interferes with all of a person's relationships. It is a frequent source of marital problems and hinders relationships with extended family members, friends, and colleagues. Unfortunately, although persons closest to someone under stress may be aware of the stress level and its effects on the person, other family members and friends may not know how much stress he or she is under and may not understand why the person has become so hostile. Thus, stress can be a "silent killer" of relationships.

Health problems

Any time people attempt to more than they can handle, physically or emotionally, they are at risk for stress-related medical problems. Excessive stress in one's daily life has been associated with a variety of health problems. Among those problems are obesity, hypertension, skeletal disorders (e.g., spinal pain, joint pain, jaw disorders), chronic headaches, systemic disorders (e.g., fibromyalgia, chronic fatigue syndrome), heart disease, and diseases of the stomach and intestinal tract.

People differ greatly in their tolerance for stress, as well as the level of stress they feel while doing specific tasks. It does not really matter whether or not one "has the time" to do all the things one has committed oneself to do. In fact, some people who have high tolerance for stress happily "jam" their days with tasks. They perform those tasks without significant problems to themselves or others. Although some people can tolerate many tasks and a great deal of stress of their daily lives, many others cannot. People must learn how much stress they can handle and the amount of stress they feel when performing various tasks in daily life.

Managing Stress

There are many ways to unburden yourself of excessive commitments and, thus, excessive stress. They are easy to learn but difficult to follow consistently. However, they work if you faithfully follow them. Some stress management practices are described below.

Know your stress limits

Take time to learn how much stress you can handle. Be honest with yourself about the amount of stress you can tolerate and continue to function as you and your loved ones want you to function each day. Can you handle higher levels of stress compared to the stress tolerance of others you know? Or do you tend to develop problems at relatively lower stress levels. Keep in mind that it is pointless to compete with others' stress tolerances.

An assessment of your stress limits also requires an examination of your life goals. Are your goals realistic, given what you want in life and the level of stress you can tolerate (or the level you believe that you can learn to tolerate)?

Say "no"

When you are asked to do something that you do not have the time or energy to do, it will raise your stress to levels you may not be able to tolerate. In such cases, be assertive! Politely, but firmly, say no to those requests.

It may be difficult to say no to requests in certain situations, such as your job. If you consistently are requested to perform tasks that *genuinely* overburden your work time, it may be necessary to discuss with your boss the fact that his or hr expectations may be excessive. Unfortunately, if your boss continues to make excessive requests, you may be forced to choose between finding another job or reducing your commitments in other areas of your life so you can assume the demands of your work.

Make time for leisure

It is very important for your stress management and, thus, your anger management that you take time for yourself, either alone or with loved ones. There are many ways to enjoy "down time." Develop a hobby, pursue a social cause, spend time with family and friends. All of these pursuits relieve stress and broaden your worldview.

Practice good health

Effective stress management is enhanced when people work to maintain their physical, as well as mental, health. Illnesses exert stress o n bodily systems, thus, increasing mental stress and poorer control of emotions. Every teenager and young adult should have a physical examination with blood chemistry every two years. Adults in midlife and older should have a physical examination with blood chemistry at least every two years or as advised by their physician. In addition, everyone should commit themselves to the following health practices:

- Eat properly. Eat plenty of fruit and vegetables. Avoid more than very small amounts of sugar, salt, caffeine, and saturated fats.
- Get enough sleep, eight hours a night. You may think you need (or can get by with) less sleep, but psychological research during the past 20 years strongly suggests that teenagers need eight to 10 hours of sleep nightly, and adults need seven or eight hours.
- Keep your weight under control. Keep your body mass index (BMI) no higher than your physician's recommended level.
- Get plenty of exercise. Walk, do aerobics, or engage in a similar light to moderate workout at least 20 minutes, three times a week.
- Avoid excessive amounts of alcohol. Drink no more than an ounce of alcohol a day. If possible, avoid alcohol altogether. In fact, if you have ever had a substance abuse problem, you should never drink alcohol again in your life!

- Avoid all other nonprescribed drugs.
- Do not smoke and, if you smoke now, take responsibility to quit. Make no excuses to avoid quitting. Select a smoking cessation program and a physician to supervise it, and follow it faithfully.

A Plan for Making Lifestyle Changes

You will need an organized plan to make the changes needed for a selfless lifestyle. Without a plan, attempts to make major changes in one's life often fail. Each failure makes it more difficult to successfully attempt to make those changes later. A good change plan has several parts, which are as follows:

1. *Goals*: A goal is a broad statement of the change you want to make in your life. You may want to develop a new personal characteristic (e.g., patience, empathy), learn a new behavior, or rid yourself of an undesired behavior or characteristic (e.g., disrespect of others). A change plan should have at least one goal.

2. *Objectives*: Objectives sometimes are called *subgoals* because they relate directly to one of the goals in a plan. Objectives are outcomes you want to achieve on the way to achieving a goal. Whereas goals are broad statements of a planned outcome in a change plan, objectives are much more specific. For example, in order to achieve the goal of empathy, you want to achieve several objectives. One of those objectives might be to clearly and consistently communicate that you correctly hear others' opinions in discussions. A second objective might be to consistently communicate understanding of another's point of view during every discussion or disagreement for

Relaxation and Stress Management

at least a month. Both of these objectives, when they are achieved, will bring you closer to the overall goal of exhibiting empathy as a personal characteristic. Make sure that every goal in your plan is accompanied by at least two objectives.

3. *Actions*: Actions are the steps you will take in order to achieve objectives. Actions, like objectives, should be as specific as possible and describe what you will do to achieve the objective. For example, in order to achieve the objective, "I will communicate understanding of another's point of view during every discussion for the next month," the action plan may be, "When I am having a disagreement with someone, I will restate what they have expressed as their point of view on the subject of our disagreement, before I state (or restate) my point of view." Every objective in a change plan should have at least one action to achieve it.

4. *Time Line*: For each objective, state the length of time you have allotted to achieve the objective (e.g., six months from today, next week). Then state the length of time or target date you have set for achieving the goal.

A chart to make a lifestyle change plan is provided in Appendix B.

Reflection Questions

1. As you began to use the progressive relaxation program, what did find easiest and most difficult about the procedure. Have you been able to adapt it to make it more effective for you?

2. As you have made progress in using the programs, how has your daily life changed? Discuss with your support person or a trusted friend ways that increased relaxation has affected the following areas of your daily life: (a) quality of sleep, (b) mood, (c) ability to manage strong emotions, (d) quality of relationships with family and friends, (e) quality of work (or school), and (f) overall quality of life.

3. Consider the health practices described in this chapter. Which ones do you practice now? Which might you need to work on? With your support person or a friend, prepare a lifestyle change plan for making positive changes in those areas that you want to improve. For each area, establish at least one clear goal, with accompanying objectives and actions using the guidelines presented in this chapter. Create a time line for completing each action plan. Remember to be realistic with your time line, allowing enough time to achieve each goal.

Chapter 8
Case Examples

Gil

Gil, 32, was referred to my clinic by the local probation department. Gil recently had been convicted of disorderly conduct and reckless driving after an episode of road rage. He had become angry when a driver cut him off after passing him. Gil chased the other driver and attempted to push him off the road by striking the rear of the car with his front bumper. Another driver in the area saw the incident and notified the police, who quickly identified Gil's car and arrested him. As a condition of his probation, Gil was required to attend anger management counseling.

During our first session, Gil acknowledged that he had been having anger problems for many years. He recalled that, on several occasions, he had "chased down" cars on the road during fits of road rage. On one occasion, he succeeded in pulling a car to the side of the road and cracked the driver's window with a broom handle. Gil also admitted that he often lost his temper over minor slights, such as receiving slow service in stores and restaurants, and when family members and colleagues did not perform tasks in the manner he thought they should be performed. When he lost his temper, he shouted and insulted the person with whom he was angry. Often, he became so angry that he destroyed things. His spouse had left him twice over his anger outbursts and he had lost a job due to aggressive behavior at work.

Gil recalled that, as a boy, his father was a raging alcoholic who spent much of the family's income on whisky and women other than Gil's mother. When he was home, Gil's father was usually loud and abusive with his words. Sometimes he was physically abusive to Gil, his brothers, and his mother. Gil recalled that he never knew what to expect when he came home from school or other activities, since he did not know his father's condition until he came into the house. He also recalled many times when his father let him down by failing to show for important events, such as ball games, awards ceremonies at school, and even Gil's high school graduation. Gil often felt like life was mostly out of his control and he could only wait for the next disappointment without being able to do anything about it. He learned that, in his words, "You can't expect anything, and you can't expect anyone to come though on anything for you." Gil had learned to believe that he must control the world around him to prevent his life from feeling chaotic.

In adolescence, Gil's temper began to become apparent to those around him, although Gil was mostly unaware of it. He often lost his temper over minor slights and when others made mistakes, even minor ones, on projects at school or at the restaurant where he worked. More troubling was that his anger always was a rage, during which he would shout very hurtful things. He called others vulgar names and threatened to strike them. On a few occasions, when the person with whom he was angry would shout back, Gil would initiate a fight.

After he married, he often called his spouse names and shouted at her when he believed she had made a mistake or did not perform a task the way he believed it should be performed. By the time he was seen in the clinic, he was in his third marriage, as his first two spouses had divorced him over his temper. He had lost two jobs and had been suspended twice for aggressive behavior in his third job. He was on legal probation for assaulting a co-worker. Generally, he was danger of losing his marriage, job, and friends and going to jail if he not learn to control his temper.

Using the anger management model described in Chapter 4, Gil learned that, as he became angry, his arms and lower back became tense and he developed a lump in his throat. He learned that, as these physical changes came over him, he was telling himself sentences such as the following:

"I'm not in control, this isn't going the way I know it's supposed to go. I've got to get him (her) straightened out. Why is he (she) not getting it? I've got to do something!"

After repeating these and similar messages to himself, Gil found that he was shouting and even physically trying to get control of the situation. He was in a rage but unable to stop his thoughts or actions.

Gil had some difficulty coming up with alternate self-messages. His need for control was quite strong and it was hard for him to let go of his rather intense resentment toward his father and his belief that it was his duty to manage all situations around him.

Eventually, however, he learned and came to accept a few alternate self-statements. They included the following:

1. "I don't have to have things go my way in all situations"

2. "This situation does not need to go my way."

3. "(*The other person' name*) is doing this fine. Back off him (her)."

Using self-stimulation (i.e., snapping his wrist with a rubber band at his spouse's request during the early moments of an argument), Gil was able to trigger the anger control steps and replace his "need for control" thoughts with his alternate thoughts. He worked with the model and used a progressive relaxation program at least twice a day. Gil was able to approach situations much more calmly in six weeks after beginning his anger management counseling. His progress was good enough to help him complete his probation without further incidents and improve his performance at work.

Margo

Margo, 38, was referred to my clinic by her doctor, who requested that she be evaluated for a possible intermittent explosive disorder. As Margo described her past experiences, she did, indeed, sound like a bomb always ready to explode with just a bit of prodding. Margo was married and the mother of four children, ages six to 15. For the past six years, she had been having severe problems with her temper. Slight disruptions in her daily routine or typical mischief by her younger children would result in her having bouts of screaming, breaking things, and rushing to her bedroom in tears. Her spouse reported that small arguments between them quickly became quarrels that led to his having to leave the house and sleep in the garage that night. Her husband also stated that Margo dwelled on conflicts for several days after they occurred, although she dropped the matter completely once she eventually got over her anger. At her job as a receptionist for a cable television company, Margo reportedly took offense easily, became intensely angry when given constructive criticism, and held grudges against coworkers who offended her.

As she described her situation, it became clear that Margo was under a great deal of stress every day. The family was in financial distress. Their home was a three-bedroom ranch style house that was too small for the family and offered little privacy. Margo was working a full time job outside her home in addition to her full time job as housekeeper, wife, and mother to four children. Neither the children nor her spouse seemed to be much help around the house. Margo's in-laws were often at the house and often criticized her for not being a stay-at-home mom, not keeping the house clean enough, and not being a good parent for a variety of trivial reasons. Margo admitted that she felt tense and anxious throughout almost every day. She told me that she wished that she did not have to go to work each day then, once the work day was over, wished she did not have to go home.

Margo's angry thinking centered around the notion of maintaining control in order to survive. Her thoughts centered around the theme, " I must have control in order to cope. " If her husband or one of the children made a mistake on a household task, she thought, "I'll lose it or go crazy if this tasks is not done right the first time." Or, when the children were fighting, her self-talk consisted statements such as, "The noise is driving me nuts! I must stop it or I'll lose control of myself!"

In counseling, Margo and I agreed that the first step in managing her anger was to reduce the stress in her daily life. With her family's involvement, Margo developed a list of tasks to be performed by each family member. She and her spouse also created a simple system of rewards for family members (spouses included) when they performed their assigned household jobs, as well as consequences when they did not perform those jobs. The reward system was useful for encouraging family members to perform their jobs consistently. Although several adjustments in assigned jobs and rewards were required for the system to work at its best, Margo's family did help heart home and this reduced the stress in her life a great deal. In addition, Margo was able to confront her in-laws with her husband's support. They worked through their conflicts to a degree that pleasantly surprised Margo and led to an improvement in her relationship with them. Margo realized that, since childhood, she had never been able to tell others what she needed from them and hated conflict. She attributed this to her memories of a father who had served in the military for several years and demanded unquestioning obedience from Margo, her three brothers, and her mother. With the encouragement of her husband and counselor, Margo worked through resentment of her father's domineering parenting style. This, in turn, enabled her to let go of her need to have full control over the way her family carried out tasks and freed her to express what she needed them to do in order to help her remain calm. Although Margo needed to use the nine-step anger management program in order to control her temper for the first few weeks of treatment, she eventually was able to get her anger under good control with these lifestyle changes.

Jim

Jim, 32, was referred by the probation department after his conviction for assault on an employee at a local discount department store. He had a previous conviction for domestic battery (striking his spouse). As part of his probation agreement, he was to receive at least six months of anger management counseling.

At our initial session, Jim made no secret that he was a very angry man. He told me in a rather eerily calm manner that, in his words, "A man runs the show and keeps it together." Jim had several rigidly-held notions about what a man was supposed to be like. One notion was that, "A man rights the ship by whipping ass. A fellow who can't do that is a woman with a penis."

Another notion was that, "A woman needs a man to set her straight, and most of the time, that means a slap across the mouth. And, a man who can't do that, well, I already told you what *he* is."

Jim went through his life at a slow burn, always ready to "be a man" with whoever was around. Although he had only two assault convictions against him, he had been in several fights and was known to some around town as a "bar buster," one who seemed always ready to fight.

During our first few counseling sessions, Jim willingly shared with me how he arrived at his beliefs about manhood and the desirability of violence as a way to solve problems. As a child, his father had the same ideas and taught them directly to Jim. If Jim did not live by those beliefs, he was punished severely. For example, if he backed away from a fight started by a peer and his father learned of it, he would spank Jim with a severity that clearly would be considered physically abusive. Jim's father beat his mother on several occasions and told Jim and his brothers that, "God intended that men keep women in line."

Early in his counseling, I confronted Jim about his ideas on men and women and challenged him to reconsider them. I think he tried to challenge his own thinking at first. He was successful in creating new thoughts about what a man would in a conflict and alternative behaviors based on his new thoughts. However, at Step 4 of the short term anger management model, commitment to acting on those new ways of thinking and behavior, he refused to continue his anger management program. Instead, he notified his probation officer that he would prefer to go to jail than give up his "manliness." As a result, he served eight months (six months and an additional 60 days for assaulting another inmate during his original sentence) in the county jail.

Looking back, I think Jim believed that changing his ideas about how a man should behave would, in effect, be a kind of disloyalty to his father. Loyalty was an important quality in his family of origin. Sadly, this loyalty prevented Jim from avoiding the same kinds of problems (job failure, criminal charges, relationship problems) that burdened his father. Equally sadly, Jim had a son who was learning the same attitudes and, from an early age, exhibited the same aggressive behaviors at school and in his neighborhood.

I share this third case to make a point. Techniques such as the ones in this book are not magic. No set of techniques, no counseling, no intervention can make people change their thinking or behavior unless people *want* to change. Jim demonstrated that he *knew how* to change his thinking and behavior. He knew how the anger management techniques worked. He was *not willing* to change and chose jail over change. As I mentioned in the first chapter and will mention again in the epilogue, you must be willing to make the effort needed to change in order to manage your anger successfully in the short term and the long term.

Reflection Questions

1. In what ways are you similar to the people described in this chapter? In what ways are you different? Was there a particular case in the chapter that you found most helpful. Why was that case helpful?

2. Make up your own case example, using yourself as the central character in the case. Describe the problems you have had managing your anger. Then describe how you have used (or plan to use) the short term and long term anger management steps in this book to develop your selfless lifestyle. Describe an outcome of the case that you are going to bring about.

Epilogue

I hope that, as you work on using the techniques in this book, you will begin to enjoy a variety of improvements in your life. Processing anger constructively may have positive effects on your health, by exerting less stress on your cardiovascular and gastrointestinal systems, reducing nervous system disturbances (e.g., headaches, spinal and body pain), and improving your mental state. Your relationships will improve and you will find your family life is more productive. You may experience more success at work, school, and social endeavors.

I want to remind you of Jim's case in the preceding chapter. Jim failed at anger management, not because he could not learn to manage his anger, but because he chose not to manage it. The small number of my past clients who did not complete my program successfully made the same choice Jim made. There are two reasons people choose not to change.

First, they may choose to believe that they cannot change. They choose instead to join the *I Can't Club*. Members of this club insist that their actions are beyond their control and there is nothing they can do to change they ways they think, feel, and act. Frankly, they tend to frustrate and annoy everyone who must deal with them or try to help them. No one cares to associate with people who whine that they are out of control of their lives.

The second reason is that people believe their ideas are the only ones that can be right. This reason applied to Jim's case. He was unwilling to believe that ideas his father did not teach could be right. Basically, Jim wasn't willing to get over himself.

If you have not done so already, I encourage you to make a commitment, right now, that you will refuse to accept membership in the *I Can't Club*. Please decide right now that you will confront yourself and let others confront you about your beliefs. Decide right now that there are other ways of thinking about people and situations in your life that are better than some ways of thinking you have now. Make the commitment to a selfless lifestyle. Make no excuses not to commit.

It will not be easy. In fact, managing your anger may be one of the most difficult things you have done in your life this far. It will take time and much practice in order to use the techniques in this book with consistent effectiveness. Achieving a selfless lifestyle requires unlearning attitudes and behaviors that one has acquired over a lifetime, and this requires time. So, be patient. If you should make mistakes while learning to use these techniques, please do not despair. Simply recommit to using them and reassure yourself that you *will* succeed!

Appendix A

SWaTAT Worksheet

Step 1: Identify the physical cues that you are angry.

What kinds of physical feelings (e.g., tightness in chest, lump in throat, hot flashes) do you feel as you become angry? How do those sensations change as you get more angry? As you get uncontrollably angry? Write them on the lines below. Be specific!

_____

_____

_____

Step 2: Determine what you are telling yourself that is making you uncontrollably angry in situations where you lose control, and what you did.

Identify your thinking that leads you to lose control when you are angry. Bring to mind one or two recent (within the past two weeks) situations where you exhibited poor management of your anger. Write them down below. Again, be very specific when describing them.

_____

_____

_____

_____

Now, remember exactly you did after you had the angry self-talk you recalled above. Ideally, your description of what you did should specific enough that readers could "see" you do it in their imaginations!

_____

_____

_____

Step 3: Think of other thoughts that would not have led to such anger in those situations and actions that would go with those thoughts.

Now think about what you could have said to yourself instead, that would have led to your remaining in control in each of those situations. These alternate thoughts cast the situation about which you were angry, in a more positive way. Write down your specific alternate thoughts.

_____

_____

_____

Now, think of the action or actions you would take if you told yourself the things you have written above, rather than what you usually tell yourself. Write them down.

_____

_____

_____

Step 4: Respond to the following question: Would you be willing to "force" yourself to think these new thoughts and use the new behaviors the next time you're angry at something or someone?

YES   NO

If your answer is "yes," then write each new thoughts and behaviors on a 4 X 6 index card as soon as possible. Keep the card in your pocket, wallet, or other convenient place at all times. Refer to it at least *five times* throughout the day between rising and retiring, whether you are angry or not, but at least three times when you are not angry. *If your answer was "no," you are finished.* This anger management program will not work for you.

For Step 8: Who is the friend or support person you will call in Step 8 (**A**ccess a Friend). Write this person's name below. Place a check mark by the name when you have gotten that person's agreement to help you in this process.

Appendix B
Lifestyle Change Planning Chart

This chart may be lengthened as needed.

My Lifestyle Change Plan

Goal 1:

_____

_____

Objective 1a:

_____

_____

Action 1a:

_____

_____

Time Line1a: This objective will be achieved on (Date):_____

Objective 1b:

_____

_____

Action 1b:

_____

_____

Time Line 1b: This objective will be achieved on (Date):_____

(*Add objectives, action, and time lines as needed*)

Goal 2: _____

_____

Objective 2a: _____

_____

Action 2a: _____

_____

Time Line 2a: This objective will be achieved on (Date): _____

Objective 2b: _____

_____

Action 2b: _____

_____

Time Line 2b: This objective will be achieved on (Date): _____

(*Add objectives and actions as needed*)

    Simply add more sections like those above, for additional goals.

About the Author

Floyd F. Robison (also known as Flip to friends and colleagues) is an associate professor in the Counseling and Counselor Education Program, School of Education, at Indiana University, on the Indianapolis (IUPUI) campus. He teaches courses on individual, family, and group counseling assessment and interventions. His research interests include the study of group counseling processes, psychological assessment techniques, and counseling older adults. He has authored more than 20 journal articles and book chapters on those topics.

Dr. Robison received his doctorate from Indiana University. He previously was a faculty member in the Department of Psychology and Mental Health Services at the University of Minnesota, Duluth and the Department of Counseling Psychology at Ball State University. He also is a Health Service Provider in Psychology in Indiana. He maintains a private practice, providing psychological assessment, individual and family therapy, and mental health services for older persons. He has provided individual and small group anger management counseling since 1988. His clients include persons referred by probation departments, social service agencies, medical clinics, and religious organizations.

Robison has received several awards for his professional and academic work. These awards in include the IMHCA Outstanding Mental Health Counselor Award (1991), ICES Counselor Educator Award (1992), Robert Shellhammer Teaching Award (1992), and other teaching awards. He is a Fellow of the Association for Specialists in Group Work and has served national professional organizations on numerous committees and task forces.

Dr. Robison is married (Beth) and has three children (Paul Blanford, Melissa, Chuck). He and Beth hand-built their home in Brown County, Indiana. In his spare time, he enjoys bluegrass music and plays several acoustic instruments with local groups.

Index

A

abdicating responsibility · 30
Action Delay Technique · 67
Actions · 92
affirmation ritual · 64
Anger · 9, 10, 11, 12, 14, 18, 19, 24, 25, 33, 36, 37, 59, 68
anger journal · 68
anger management · 9, 11, 13, 14, 25, 31, 33, 36, 39, 41, 43, 44, 45, 46, 47, 68, 75, 85, 89, 94, 96, 97, 100, 101, 102, 104, 108, 112
Anger Management Quiz · 10
angry attitudes · 24, 36
angry self talk · 24
anxiety · 13, 19, 31, 86
appetite problems · 13
arousal · 18, 21, 22, 26

B

Beck, Aaron · 19, 23
bipolar disorder · 32
body breathe · 79

C

chronic fatigue syndrome · 87
confidence · 51, 56, 66
consequences of anger · 12
corrective behavioral feedback statemen · 72
counseling · 25, 31, 32, 33, 41, 43, 94, 97, 99, 100, 101, 102, 112
cue 38, 42

cue word 38

D

deferral · 66
depression · 13, 31, 32, 86

diseases of the stomach · 87
Dropping the charges · 61

E

emotional reaction · 72
Empathy · 49, 91

F

feedback message · 71, 72, 73, 74
feeling words · 73
fibromyalgia · 87
Frank · 28

G

Gil · 94
goal · 47, 66, 67, 68, 77, 91, 92, 93

H

Health problems · 87
heart disease · 87
human emotions · 9, 18
Humility · 52, 55
Humor · 53, 68

I

Immediacy · 49
Impulse control disorders · 32
Intermittent Explosive Disorder · 32
interpersonal feedback · 71

J

Jane · 26
Janet · 27
Jim · 100

L

leisure · 89
Letting Go · 59
limbic system · 18
low sexual desire · 87

M

mania · 32
manic-depressive disorder · 32
Margo · 97
memory and thinking disorders · 13
Mental handicaps · 33

O

Objectives · 91

P

Patience · 52, 55
personality disorder · 32
positive feedback · 74
progressive relaxation · 77, 78, 85, 86, 93, 97
psychiatric medications · 33
Psychological Problems · 31
psychologists · 11, 19, 30, 77
psychosis · 33
Psychotic disorders · 33

Q

quarrel · 10, 69, 70
quiet place · 79, 80, 81, 82, 83, 84

R

Rapid Relaxation Technique · 85
Reflection Questions · 15, 23, 34, 45, 58, 74, 92
Relationship problems · 87
requested behavior change · 72
respect · 25, 28, 48, 50, 66
responsibility · 15, 24, 29, 30, 31, 34, 51, 57, 72, 91
road rage · 11

S

say no · 89
schizophrenia · 33
self-confidence · 29
self-discipline · 11
selfish thinking style · 24
selfishness · 12, 26, 27, 28, 29, 30
selfless attitudes · 14
Selfless people · 13, 50, 51, 52, 53
selfless thinking style · 13, 14
selflessness · 47, 48, 49, 50, 66
self-stimulation · 97
self-talk · 14, 19, 21, 22, 23, 25, 28, 29, 34, 36, 37, 38, 47, 53, 55, 107
Sexual problems · 86
sleep problems · 13
stress · 11, 77, 86, 87, 88, 89, 90, 98, 99, 104
Stress Management · 77, 85
subgoals · 91
Support Persons · 43
SWaTAT · 36, 37, 40, 41, 106

T

Time Line · 92, 110, 111
Tom · 26
Trust · 50, 51

www.ingramcontent.com/pod-product-compliance
Lightning Source LLC
Chambersburg PA
CBHW020012050426
42450CB00005B/434